Tadeusz Dajczer

THE GIFT OF FAITH

In the Arms of Mary
FOUNDATION
COMMUNION OF LIFE WITH CHRIST THROUGH MARY

Fourth American Edition

Original Title: **Rozważania o wierze**
Previously printed in English as **Inquiring Faith**
Imprimatur: +Most Rev. Christopher Jones, Bishop of Elphin

Published by
In the Arms of Mary Foundation
P.O. Box 271987
Fort Collins, CO 80527-1987
E-mail address: inquiry@IntheArmsofMary.org
Website: www.IntheArmsofMary.org

Edited by
Anne Mary Hines   Mary Jane Bartee   Erin Rice
Michelle Curtis   Joyce Pfaffinger   Andree Wagatha

Cover and text design by
Ewa Krepsztul

Cover Image: Baptismal Font Vintage @ VectorStock.com/19002336
Used with permission.

"Decalogue for Faith Sharing" from Families of Nazareth Movement USA.
Used with permission.

In loving memory of Anne Mary Hines — our committed co-editor and past President of the In the Arms of Mary Foundation. As God's willing instrument of grace, her witness of faith showed us a sincere example of following the road to communion of life with Christ through Mary. Pray for us, beloved daughter of Mary!
- The Publishing Team

Fourth American Edition
ISBN: 978-1-93-331460-0

CONTENTS

Appendix

PART ONE

THE VIRTUE
OF FAITH

F aith, what does it mean? The theological virtue of faith is particularly complex. Presented herein, the reality of faith is understood, not in terms of dogmatic theology, but in terms of the theology of spiritual life. The faith of the New Testament is man's response to the revelation of God in Jesus Christ. Faith is participation in the Divine life. It is experiencing God's life within us which allows us to see ourselves and the reality surrounding us as if we were seeing it through the eyes of God. It is the adherence to Christ, our Master, our Lord, our Friend. It permits us to rely on Christ, the never failing rock of our salvation, and to entrust ourselves to His infinite power and boundless love. In the face of our human helplessness, faith becomes the continuous resort to the limitless mercy of God and the awaiting of everything from Him. (Gustave Thils, *Christian Holiness: A Precis of Ascetical Theology*, trans. John L. Farrand [Tielt, Belgium: Lannoo Publishers, 1961], 370, 371.)

CHAPTER ONE

FAITH AS PARTICIPATION IN THE LIFE OF GOD

S t. Thomas Aquinas says that faith brings us closer to God's knowledge of reality. **By sharing in God's life, we start to see and evaluate everything as if through His eyes** – *omnia quasi oculo Dei intuemur.*[1]

Sharing in God's life through faith causes us to become a new person; we obtain a new comprehension of reality, a new perception of God, as well as a new perception of the temporal reality around us. Through faith we begin to perceive in temporal reality the actions of the first cause – the works of God. We notice His presence and work within ourselves as well as in the world of nature and history. We notice that He is the author and creator of everything. We realize that what we come to know only in human and

---

[1] Thils, *Christian Holiness*, 371; Thomas Aquinas, *In Boeth de Trinitate*, q. 3, a.1.

worldly terms is not complete reality; it is seeing merely the surface, seeing only the secondary causes that God employs.

Faith is a virtue that allows us to be in touch with God, and is fundamental to supernatural life. Since faith is fundamental to all supernatural works, everything happens because of it. The positive qualities or shortcomings of our faith determine the activity of our supernatural life. Difficulties in supernatural life always stem from a weakness of faith. Faith is the basic virtue since it gives us the possibility of sharing in the life of God. Faith is a sharing in God's thinking. It is as if supernatural reason were placed upon the natural faculties of the soul. Faith allows us to think as God does, not only about ourselves, but also about everything we come in contact with. Therefore, to have faith means to synchronize our thought with His thought and to identify ourselves with His thought.

The difference between knowing naturally and knowing through faith is not merely a difference of degree, but is the essence of the matter. Faith brings about our unity with God's thinking and an internal sharing in the light by which God knows Himself. In this sense, it leads to contemplation and is an introduction to the future knowledge of God in eternal life.

Since it is through faith that we penetrate into the life of God, into the life of Jesus Christ, then it is through this same faith that God begins His own life within us. The purpose of our faith is for us to think as Jesus Christ does – to allow Him, who is living in us through faith, to use us, think within us, and live in us.

Because faith can accomplish a complete change in us from our former way of seeing, thinking, feeling, and experiencing, it changes our mentality. It tells us to always place God first, to be concerned about focusing our entire life on Him, and to interpret the world in the divine light coming from God. Then the light of faith illuminates all of our judgments, appraisals, desires, and expectations. In this way communion of faith is brought about, communion that will realize its fullness only in love.

The created world surrounding us is a voice that speaks to us. If our faith is weak, then that voice will distract us, pull us away from God, and will focus our attention on itself. As faith grows, the opposite process occurs. The outside world begins to speak of God, to focus our attention on God, to draw us to Him, to become a sign of His presence, to help us get in touch with Him, and to become a place where we encounter Him.

Faith enables us to overcome pretenses and to see the primary cause above secondary causes. It allows us to see that all that happens around us does not happen due to man's power. Faith allows us to discover the traces of God in creation. It gives us the ability to perceive God's will in phenomena and to see events as signs of God passing by.

TO PERCEIVE THE LOVING PRESENCE

Every moment of our lives is permeated with the Presence that loves and bestows. To live in faith means to be able to see this loving and constantly bestowing Presence. Because of faith, Christ gradually becomes a light that shines through a person's whole life and that shines through the world. He becomes a living, active presence in the life of His disciples. Every moment of our lives brings us His presence. Time is the Presence written with a capital "P." It is the presence of Christ in our lives. It is the personal presence of God, revealing Himself as the One who expects something from us. God reveals Himself to us through His will. But what is His will? It is always that which is best for us because God is Love. **Every moment of your life is a moment of meeting with the Presence that is loving you.** Someone has said that time is the sacrament of the meeting between man and God. This means that every moment is an evangelical gift since it is the Presence that calls us to do something. God links grace to each moment, be it an easy or difficult one. St. Paul says that we live, move, and exist in God (cf. Acts 17:28). It is from Him that we therefore receive not only the gift of our existence, but also the gifts of breathing, food, friendship, and the gift of every moment of our lives.

The statement of St. Thérèse of the Child Jesus that "everything is grace"[2] (*tout est grace*) means that everything that happens in your life is linked with some kind of grace. God comes to you in the form of a gift, in the form of grace, in the form of a call. In this sense, everything is a grace. God wants everything to become for you a "capital" of good. He even tries to draw good out of evil. Evil cannot be a grace, but God, in His almighty and infinite mercy, can even draw good from it. The consequences of evil can give fruit in the form of a great opportunity to be converted. Therefore, "everything is grace," and everything is a "gift," since always

---

[2] "The Yellow Notebook of Mother Agnes," June 5, 1897 in *St. Thérèse of Lisieux: Her Last Conversations*, trans. John Clarke (Washington, DC: ICS Publications, 1977), 57.

and everywhere God gives you an opportunity. It is extremely important for you to believe in this constant Presence who manifests Himself in various ways.

The present moment — each moment — brings love, as Stefan Cardinal Wyszynski has said.[3] Grace is the expression of love, so every moment is linked to God's love since it is linked with His grace. Even when you commit a grievous sin Christ is with you and loves you. If you remembered this, if you believed that you are always immersed in the merciful love of God who never abandons you, then it is certain that you would never fall.

Everything that you experience is linked to the love of God who loves you, and to His desire for your good. He is present in your life no matter what you do. Time is a sacrament of your meeting with God and His mercy, with His love for you and His desire that everything work toward your good. Then every fault becomes a "happy fault" (*felix culpa*). If you looked at every moment of your life in this way, then spontaneous prayer would be born within you. It would be a continuous prayer since the Lord is always with you and always loves you. Every moment of your life would be permeated with the love of the Presence that always encompasses you.

TRACES OF GOD IN THE WORLD

Faith allows us to notice the traces of God's works in everything, to understand that He is present within us — in

---

[3] Cardinal Stefan Wyszynski (1901-1981) was Primate of Poland during the difficult time of communist oppression. He was persecuted and imprisoned and became the spiritual leader of the Polish nation.

our spiritual, emotional, and physical lives. **If we know how to see God in everything, our prayer will become a prayer of faith**. It will be a prayer not only of words but also a prayer of seeing and admiring the world, a prayer of gratitude for everything that God gives us. Through faith we discover that man only seems to be the protagonist in the history of the world; in reality God is the main protagonist. The presence of God throughout history affects equally the things that happen in the realm of politics, society, and the economy, as well as in our family or in professional matters. He is present everywhere, and everything depends on Him. In His hands lie the destinies of all of us, as well as the destinies of nations and of the world. We come to know all this through faith, which brings about inner peace in us. This peace flows from faith that gives us the understanding that He, Who is the eternal might and eternal love, holds everything in His hands filled with mercy. He guides everything with His eternal wisdom and total love. Faith gives us feelings of security and peace, and the confidence that we are **always immersed in God's love**. Faith is a different way of looking at the world, another way of seeing that which is especially difficult. Faith allows us to come to know God in the phenomena of nature in which we can continually discover the traces of His works and the traces of His concern for us and the world that surrounds us.

St. Francis was a man of great faith who saw traces of God in everything. What incredible faith comes through the attitude of Francis when he prays with the words: "Praise to You, Lord, through Sister Moon and the stars. Praise to You, Lord, through Brothers Wind and Air." Did it ever happen, while you were walking through a meadow or forest in which the wind blew, that you felt the gentle touch of God in that wind? If so, there is within you something of the faith of St. Francis of Assisi, who saw a sign of God's work in everything. *Praise to You, Lord, through Brother Wind; praise to You Who is in this wind. Praise to You for this air that refreshes us, which we can breathe, for You are our breath and our air.* Everything comes from the Lord – good times and bad. Bad weather is also His weather. Living faith permits us to see God's miracles in the world around us, in our ordinary, everyday lives. Even murky weather and rain are miracles performed for us by God. Rain, which has certainly soaked us more than once, is the Lord's touch. If you see this, that will be your **prayer of faith.**

Praise to you, Lord, through Sister Water. By drinking water when we are thirsty, especially on hot and sweltering days, we can experience the presence of the Lord. We are not accustomed to looking at the world this way. But in this ordinary, everyday situation we can see God who, through this water, refreshes us and moistens our dry, parched lips. He is in that water. The realization of this Presence is the foundation of faith. That is why St. Francis reminds us of "Sister Water," a symbol of God's presence and work.

TALENTS

God waits for us to look with the eyes of faith at all the experiences we live through, especially the difficult ones. In the parable of the talents, Jesus warns us not to close ourselves off from coming to know Him through faith, and not to be slothful in using all the things that God is continuously giving us. Upon leaving five talents with the first servant, two with the second one, and one with the third (see Mt 25-14-30), and obliging them to work, the Master gave them an opportunity. The word "talent," which during Christ's time signified a certain monetary value, now signifies an intellectual "value." We say that someone is a talented musician or talented mathematician. The meaning of the parable about the talents is, however, much more profound. Evangelical thinking is like turning our worldly, purely human thinking inside out. This is also the case in the parable about the talents. A talent is a gift and a particular raw material, and at the same time an opportunity. **Christ, in giving you a talent, trusts you and waits for you to take proper advantage of it.** If He has given you certain abilities, He is not indifferent about what you do with them. However, if you have not received these abilities, this is also a talent. **A talent is not only receiving something, but it is also lacking something.**

In the light of faith, the good health you have is a talent, but bad health is also a talent. In each case Jesus poses the question, *What are you doing with this talent?* You can waste health and, even more so, a lack of health. **Everything is a gift; a talent is a gift.** God continuously bestows gifts on you. It is a talent, for example, if you are unable to pray; yet you consider this to be a misfortune. It is important what you do with this inability to pray. Maybe you have buried this talent and you say to yourself, *Well, I will not pray.* But you can gain so much from it. The inability to pray should intensify your hunger for God and, thereby, it can become a means contributing to your sanctification. The same thing applies when you have problems at home, when the family is quarrelling, this is also your talent and an opportunity given to you by God. What can you do with it? If you break down and are discouraged, then you bury it in the ground. It is impossible for a person of faith not to see the deeper meaning of his own experiences. The very search for the deeper understanding of personal experiences is to profit from the talent. If you experience fear – for example, you fear suffering or death – this is also an opportunity offered to you. St. Thérèse of the Child Jesus had a great fear of spiders. She told how she once had to force herself to remove the spiders' webs from the alcove under the stairs.[4] This helped her greatly on her way to the Lord. Placed in her hands was a talent from which she knew how to gain profit.

If certain situations make you feel tense, it means that your talent is hidden within them, as if a diamond were buried beneath the ashes. What do you do with it? How do you make use of it? Everything is meant to serve toward your sanctification. In this sense, everything is grace. Suffering that overwhelms you, or other unfavorable circumstances, are a whole mass of talents. However, we are often like blind people or like children who understand very little. It is only when we stand before God that everything will be made clear to us. Then we will see the ocean of talents in which we have been immersed.

There are two kinds of talents: those that are less precious and those that are more precious. If you are successful, if something comes out right for you, this is certainly a talent. However, if nothing turns out right, this is a more precious talent. **Failures are the priceless treasures given to you in your**

---

[4] "Yellow Notebook," July 13, 1897 in *Thérèse: Last Conversations*, 96.

life. Just like the master in the Gospel who returned from his travels and demanded an account from his servants, God will someday ask you how you made use of your personal failures that He gave you as an opportunity, as a talent. Sometimes there are many failures in your life – do you make use of them?

The parable of the talents is an evangelical call to conversion. You have to start looking at your life differently; you must look at it with the eyes of faith. Then you will see God's endless giving of graces; you will see your whole life as a multitude of hidden opportunities for continual inner transformation. You will come to know that everything is grace. It seems that God, granting you difficult graces, is forcing His gifts into your hands, but you resist and do not want to accept them. **Yet, difficult graces are the most valuable talents of your life.** Sometimes there are many of them because God wants you to have enough talents to make use of.

Faith is sharing in God's vision of reality, but God looks at your life in a completely different way. If you have faith, it is like seeing every day of your life through the eyes of Jesus. Only then will you see the unceasing opportunities for your conversion and sanctification. Then, in the light of faith, you will also begin to understand suffering that is a cross and something that will therefore spiritually transform you to the extent that you accept it. If in your difficulties you recognize the cross as an opportunity toward transformation, then your difficulties truly become gifts for you. If you could see all the countless talents that God is continuously giving you, then you would never be sad. Talents such as poor health or situations filled with conflicts and failures would then bring joy to your heart – joy because God bestows something invaluable on you and shows you exceptional trust. He trusts that you will not bury or reject His gifts. **He counts on your faith** since it is only in the light of faith that you can recognize the talents given to you. A talent is everything that you have understood and remembered up to this moment. However, poor memory and the fact that you forget many things is also a talent because everything brings grace and – in this meaning – everything is a grace.

Only a person who has faith is able to be grateful for everything. This gratitude will be visible on your face as joy, for everything may be changed into good. This reflection about talents refers to the teaching of St. Paul and to the famous thesis of St. Augustine, "We know that all things work for good for those who love God" (Rom 8:28) – even sin. Therefore, even a fall, which is a great misfortune and at the same time hurts Jesus, can be an opportunity within which is hidden some kind of talent given to you from which you can profit. You only need your faith, or your conversion toward such faith, to enable you to see through the eyes of Jesus. He is never sad when looking at your life that may be filled with failures, problems, conflicts, unfulfilled plans, everyday difficulties, and spiritual difficulties. He is joyful because He expects all those things to bear fruit. He expects that you will take advantage of them and you will be joyful and grateful for everything He gives you: Mother Agnes said to the ailing Thérèse of the Child Jesus, "You had a lot of trouble today," and she answered, 'Yes, but since I love it . . . I love everything that God gives me.'[5]

---

[5] "Yellow Notebook," August 14, 1897 in *Thérèse: Last Conversations*, 148.

St. Bernadette looked at her life in a similar way. Her "testament" is an exceptionally expressive statement of gratitude for the gifts that she received:

For the extreme poverty of my father and mother, the failure of the mill, the wood that brought unhappiness, the wine of fatigue, the dirty sheep, thank You, my God.

For the extra mouth to be fed that I was, for the ragged children, for the sheep that I watched, thank You.

Thank You, my God, for the procurator, the superintendent of police, the policemen, and for Abbé Peyramale's harsh words!

For the days when you came, Our Lady Mary; for the days when you did not come – only in paradise can I give you thanks!

For the slap in the face, ... for the bantering, the insults, for those who believed I was crazy, for those who believed I was lying, for those who believed I was greedy, thank you, Lady Mary!

For the spelling I never learned, the knowledge of books I never had, for my ignorance and my stupidity, thank you!

Thank you! Thank you! Because had there been in this world a girl more ignorant and stupid than I, you would have chosen her.

For my mother who died so far away, for my sorrow when my father instead of opening his arms to his little Bernadette, called me "Sister Marie-Bernard," I thank You, Jesus!

Thank you for having filled with bitterness the far-too tender heart you gave me!

For Mother Josephine who said that I was good for nothing, thank You!

For the mother mistress' sarcastic remarks, for harsh words, her ridicule, and the bread of humiliation, thank You!

Thank You for making me the one to whom she could say: "You are not like all the others."

Thank You for making me the privileged recipient of her rebukes, so that my sisters used to say, "How lucky that we are not Bernadette!"

Yes, thank you, Lady Mary, that I am Bernadette, who was threatened with prison because I saw you. I am she who the crowds stared at as a rare animal – that Bernadette so wretched that upon seeing her, it was said: "Is that it?"

For this pitiful body You have given me, this illness of fire and smoke, for my rotting flesh, my riddled bones, my sweats, my fever, my dull pains and my sharp ones, thank You, my God.

And for the soul that You have given me, for the desert of interior dryness, for Your nights, for Your lightening, for Your silences and Your thunder, for everything, for You absent and for You present, thank You, Jesus. (Editor translation of Marcelle Auclair, *Bernadette*, [France: Boud et Gay, 1957]; Marcelle Auclair, *Bernadette*, trans. Kathryn Sullivan [France: Desclee, 1958], 194-195)

CHAPTER TWO

FAITH AS ADHERING TO CHRIST

F aith, in the subjective sense, is not only sharing in God's life, but is also an existential adherence to Christ as the one Lord and one Love. This implies that each person makes a choice and steers his will toward Christ as the final goal and greatest priority.

Adherence to Christ is our answer to His call and to His looking upon us with complete love. This answer will always be marked with adventure and also with risk. Jesus wants us to attach ourselves to Him without questioning details, without considering the consequences of our choice, and without questioning the future. He wants us to answer *yes* as Mary did – expressing in this way our complete abandonment to God. The essence of trustful abandonment to Jesus and adherence to Him lies in our accepting the unknown that remains in darkness and, therefore, demands faith. Adherence to Christ is the beginning of love. It will be accomplished by the merging of our will with the will of Christ. This is the beginning of our personal communion with God.

Our adherence to Christ is not possible without detaching ourselves from whatever can enslave us. The apostles, in order to follow Christ, had to leave everything. To choose Christ as the supreme value is also to consent that He Himself will form us.

"NO ONE CAN SERVE TWO MASTERS"

Faith, which is the adherence to Christ as the only Lord and our only Love, requires turning to Him as the One who is of greatest value. Total adherence to Christ requires a free heart, therefore, a turning away from being enslaved to mammon. The Gospel says, "No one can serve two masters. He will either hate one and love the other, or be devoted to one and despise the other. You cannot serve God and mammon" (Mt 6:24). There are two masters – God and mammon; there is no third. The highest authority, Jesus Christ, has said this. The relationship of one master to the other is a relationship of radical contradiction. The Gospel clearly states, "He will either hate one and love the other, or be devoted to one and despise the other" (Mt 6:24). If you love one master, you hate the other. And if you are devoted to one, then you must despise the other. This is a very strong statement. We cannot, therefore, attach ourselves to Christ and serve Him while at the same time serving mammon, even though we are always exposed to the temptation to compromise and combine that which cannot be combined.

"No one can serve two masters" (Mt 6:24). Who are these *masters* (Greek: *kyrios*)? One is Christ, our one true Lord – *Kyrios*. The other is mammon – the false *kyrios*, the false lord. To serve mammon is to enslave oneself and become dependent on some kind of material or spiritual good. Notice that mammon is called a master, who is served as one serves a king. **We either serve God and love Him and despise mammon, that is, our attachment to material and spiritual goods, or** – it is terrifying even to think – **we love our attachment to these goods and**, perhaps unconsciously, **we begin to despise God.**

If you analyze your prayer, this will help you to identify what forms and images mammon takes in your life. **If you take stock of what you are thinking about most often during prayer, then you will see what your greatest treasure is.** "For where your treasure is, there also will your heart be" (Mt 6:21). Your distractions will allow you to discover how many attachments to mammon you have. If there are many, do not be surprised that it is difficult for you to concentrate during the rosary, during adoration, or during the Eucharist.

The word *kyrios* in the Greek language means absolute ruler and master. On the other hand, the word *douleuein* (to serve) means enslaved servitude to the absolute master and complete ownership by him. The Gospel says that we belong entirely to the Lord, regardless of whether we acknowledge this or not. We are and will always remain the property of the Lord, who is Jesus.

Originally, the Hebrew term *mammon* meant some kind of treasure – money or expensive things put into a deposit. At that time, it did not have a negative meaning. In the course of time, however, an evolution in the understanding of this term came about. It started to mean that when expensive things were placed with a banker or someone of trust, one could then count on the treasure and place hope in it. This was the first step of the evolution. Mammon was becoming an object of trust. Next the word mammon started to be written with a capital letter since it already had become a false lord and master. Then an unusual alienation occurred; **a thing took possession of the person**. Everything in which he had placed his hope started to become a god for him.

And you, in whom or in what do you place your hope? What do you count on? Who is your God? If you place your hope in a false god, then you will know bitterness and disappointment, because it is a master that sooner or later will disappoint you. This will be a great grace for you because then your trust in mammon will begin to crumble.

What can this mammon that enslaves your heart be? It can be material as well as spiritual goods. For example, it can be attachment to money, to your children, to your work, or to something you are presently creating or working on. It may be attachment to peace or even to one's own perfection. All these attachments cause your bondage and bring you slavery. As a human being you can choose to attach yourself to the one and only reality – the will of God. Everything that enslaves you closes you off from God and diminishes your faith.

How can you uncover your mammon? Are the tension, stress, restlessness, rushing, and sadness that accompany you through life signs that you serve some kind of mammon? There are people, for example, who live under constant stress. How great then must be their attachment to something opposed to God. People free from attachments are filled with the peace of God. The peace of God builds and strengthens mental health, which in turn reflects on physical health. In this way, the soul, the psyche, and the body participate in a person's great freedom. A person free from attachments is also free from facial wrinkles, from stress, and from the diseases of civilization. **Mammon systematically destroys a human person**. It not only blocks your way to Christ and your adherence to Him, but it also destroys your health and your psyche.

An obvious **sign of attachments** is also your **sadness in situations when God takes something away from you**. He will, therefore, take that to which you are enslaved; hence, He will take everything that is your greatest enemy – whatever causes your heart not to be free for Him. It is only when you start to cheerfully accept these kinds of situations, and submit with serenity, that you will become more and more free.

While standing before the Lord during prayer, show Him not only your empty hands, but also your dirty hands defiled by your attachments to mammon, and pray that He will have mercy on you. Prayer can develop only in the atmosphere of freedom. As a disciple of Christ, you are especially called to contemplative prayer. **For your prayer to become contemplation** – a loving gaze on Jesus Christ, your beloved – **it is essential to have a free heart**. That is why

Christ fights so much for your heart to be free. He fights through various events, difficulties, and storms, all the while giving you the chance to cooperate intensely with grace. In all these situations, Christ expects that you will try to cleanse your heart soiled by attachments and servitude to mammon. Hence, all these difficult moments and all the storms are graces for you. They are the passing by of the Merciful Lord who loves you so much that He wants to give you this magnificent gift – **the gift of the total freedom of your heart**. Your heart should not be divided; it should be a heart solely for Him.

To have faith means to see and understand the meaning of your life in accordance with the Gospel, and that God is most important. Your life is to be oriented toward Him – primarily to seek and to build His kingdom, with faith that everything else will be given to you (cf. Mt 6:33). God wants to bestow each person with all His love. However, He can bestow this on a person only to the extent of his openness and his readiness to be stripped of his attachments so that room may be made for Him. It is faith that creates this emptiness and vacuum in us where God can dwell.

THE WILL OF GOD AND OUR OWN WILL

Whether our faith will deepen someday to the point of total adherence to Christ depends on our desire to do His will in everything, together with our consent to crucify our own will. To adhere to Christ means to surrender our will to His will. Spiritual life is brought about under continuous tension between the will of God and the will of a person. The tension comes from the fact that we revolve continuously around our will, around whatever is convenient for us, while it is obvious that the scope of our plans and desires, of what we want, does not correspond to what God wants. Man defends against anything that would be contrary to his own desires. He is either consciously defensive when he refuses to submit to the will of God, or there is a similar process happening in his subconscious, which often takes the form of a defense mechanism of his rationalization. This mechanism shows how much self-seeking there is in our desires and efforts.

What is this defense mechanism of rationalization? It is the subconscious prescribing motives acceptable to us for our own activities, while at the same time rejecting the true motives not accepted by us. Using everyday language, we could say that in our striving to achieve our hidden desires and intentions, we invent certain self-justifying theories that comfort us. A classic example that illustrates this defense system is a mother defending her son in front of her daughter-in-law. When the defense mechanism of rationalization is triggered, the mother will be completely convinced that she is acting only out of love, and that she has that right since she is his mother and wants only what is best for him. Then possessive love for her son, which usually occurs in such a case, remains hidden behind the subconscious defense mechanism and the invented subjective theory that justifies such an attitude. When the mother behaves this way, it is almost impossible to convince her that she is loving only herself through her son, that she is breaking up the marriage, and that she should step aside or even take the side of her daughter-in-law instead of supporting her son.

The defense mechanism of rationalization is such a strong *fortress* and so difficult to disarm primarily because it is in the subconscious. How often do we, every one of us, invent some theory to justify our improper behavior? We say: *After all, I must rest, I cannot take care of that; after all, I have a right to that; after all, I was hurt, I have to defend myself, etc.* **You can even be very devoted to a so-called love – to the apostolate, to honorable causes – but at the source of this may lay a hidden and subconscious egoism.**

It is egoism that causes our spiritual life to continue on within a framework of constant tension between our will and the will of God. If living by faith means adherence to Christ and to His will, then in this context it should be emphasized that seeking our own will is the worst thing we could do. It is the source of evil and sin, the source of our misfortune and enslavement. Adherence to Christ and to His will means that, when His will is not in accordance with our will, we accept His ruining our plans. We accept His foiling them. The events in the lives of the saints often show us how God foiled human plans so that the human will could unite with the will of God.

St. Teresa of Avila was traveling to Seville where she intended to found a new monastery. These were difficult times for the reform. At that time Teresa was founding a newly reformed branch of the Carmelite Sisters. The foundation of the convent in a new city required that she go there as the Superior with a group of sisters. The sisters usually traveled in well-covered wagons because the reformed Carmelite sisters, known as discalced, were cloistered nuns who could not appear in public. Hidden in the covered wagons, they felt safe and hoped that they would arrive at their destination without being seen by anyone because they did not want to cause a sensation by showing themselves.

It was Pentecost Sunday. The sisters departed very early in the morning. Teresa had chosen a church in the far suburbs of Cordoba, where they had decided to stop. The priest there, Fr. Julian of Avila, was to celebrate Mass for them so that they would not be seen, and the sisters intended to later continue their journey. Soon it became apparent that, in order to get to their chosen church, they had to cross a bridge. The bridge was closed at that early hour. The sisters learned that the key could only be issued by a senior official. However, the official was still asleep and had left orders that he must not be disturbed by such matters. Thus, they had to wait. In the meantime, the sun was rising, and it was getting hot. People were starting to gather around the wagons. Some, seeking sensation, even tried to peek into the wagons. Finally after two hours of waiting, the key was brought and the gate was opened. The wagons moved forward, but they proved to be too wide to pass through the gate of the bridge.

More hours passed. St. Teresa had wanted so much to celebrate the Feast of Pentecost at an earlier Mass, and it was very important to her that the sisters pass unnoticed. When they finally sawed off the parts of the wagons that were sticking out, and the sisters arrived at the church outside of town, they were met with yet another surprise. It turned out that the church was dedicated to the Holy Spirit and, as always on the Feast of Pentecost, there were crowds of people inside and outside the church. This was too much. St. Teresa said that she was ready to even forego Mass. The rest of the sisters were also ready to give it up. It was not until later that St. Teresa admitted that this could have been a serious mistake. Luckily, Fr. Julian directed the sisters to attend Mass despite the crowds. They came out of the security of their hiding and started to pass through the crowded church. St. Teresa – who usually had a picturesque manner of speaking – said later that when the people saw them under their veils, in their white clothes and coarse woolen capes, they reacted similar to onlookers at a bullfight when a bull comes into the arena. Teresa said this was one of the really bad moments of her life. This very bad moment in her life was granted to her by the Holy Spirit on His feast day.

This was not the end of the difficulties. After Mass, the sisters had to pass once again through the screaming and clamoring crowd, and after coming out they discovered that, because of the intense heat, they could not travel further. The horses refused to pull the wagons. Inside the wagons it was so hot and stifling that the sisters took their siesta under a bridge. None of their plans had worked out.[6]

The Holy Spirit can descend upon a person with graces that will ruin all his plans. These are His great graces of detachment. His treatment of Teresa in this manner on the day of Pentecost showed His great love for her. She had planned and set up everything so perfectly for herself, and He foiled her plans so perfectly because they were not according to His will. In all this, the most important thing

---

[6] Teresa of Avila, *The Book of Her Foundations*, vol. 3, in *The Collected Works of St. Teresa of Avila*, trans. Kieran Kavanaugh and Otilio Rodriguez (Washington, DC: ICS Publications, 1985), 226-27.

was that **the Holy Spirit "descended" on Teresa and the remaining sisters, for they accepted His works; by surrendering to the will of God, they adhered closer to Christ.** The Holy Spirit, the great Builder of our faith, stripped them and reduced them to poverty so that they could accept the strength of Him who, in the liturgy of the Church, is called "The Father of the Poor."

CHAPTER THREE

FAITH AS RELYING ON CHRIST AND ENTRUSTING OURSELVES TO HIM

F aith is participation in the life of God; it is adherence to
Him as the only Lord, as well as relying on Him alone.
Relying on Christ and totally abandoning ourselves to Him
expresses our complete confidence in Him. A person is made
to seek out a feeling of security, to seek something to rely on,
which means he is directed toward self-entrustment to God.
He is directed toward having a system of security, toward
counting on something, and entrusting himself to something
or someone. A feeling of security is the basic, most elementary
need of the human psyche. Lack of security creates fear,
whether in a threatening situation, or in a situation when

something we rely on is taken away. This fear that arises in us causes us to intensify our efforts to feel secure.

When we count on our possessions, such as money, talents, and abilities, we are referring to relying on things, and feeling secure in a material sense. We can also reinforce our feelings of security in a personal sense when we count on our contacts and interpersonal relationships aimed toward the realization of our plans. Often feeling secure in the material sense is connected with our being oriented toward the future. A person with a strong psychological resonance[7] tries to foresee in detail what will happen in the future, and tries to prepare for everything, so that he is not taken by surprise. In this way, it is as if he wants to control the future; and he seeks in this something to rely on and a feeling of security.

This kind of search for security is always present in our lives. A student taking an exam bases his security on his memory of what he has learned or on his abilities. He can also count on what is called "luck," but he will always try to rely on something, whether it is in the material or personal sense. Nevertheless, all human systems of security cannot be perfect since they are based solely on our plans or calculations; that is why they have to fail, and then a crisis comes. If you trust in yourself, in your abilities, in your possessions, or in people with whom you are connected, sooner or later you will have to be disappointed.

In order for our faith to be reliance on Christ and entrustment of ourselves to Him, we have to accept Him as

---

[7] Someone who is psychologically impressionable has many experiences that reverberate and are retained in the psyche.—Ed.

our only true security. Flowing from faith in Christ's Word, complete abandonment to Him is the only adequate response to His unfathomable love for us.

GOD – THE ONLY ONE TO RELY ON

Faith is relying on nothing apart from God. We cannot rely on any of His gifts, but only on Him alone – on His infinite power and infinite love.

A moving scene took place in the courtyard of the temple when it was God who watched people put their donations into the money box. Every few moments the clink of falling coins could be heard, while at the side Jesus Christ and His apostles were sitting and observing those offerings. A widow put two small coins worth a penny into the box, and the Lord said, "This poor widow put in more than all the other contributors…She, from her poverty, has contributed all she had, her whole livelihood" (Mk 12:43-44). We can admire her deed. She gave all, while the rich gave only from their surplus wealth. Yet, to see just her gesture is not enough. It needs to be pointed out that by giving everything, she "sentenced" herself to death since she did not have any more money and no longer had the means to live. She herself severed her material system of security – hence the amazement of God Himself as expressed through the solemn words, "Amen, I say to you,… she, from her poverty, has contributed all she had, her whole livelihood" (Mk 12:43-44). Inconceivable is the faith of this woman!

A person who is stripped of everything – his whole system of security – is left with two options: he may either despair or, through faith, completely entrust himself to God. That is the kind of faith the widow must have had. For her, God must have been everything – her only support. God can strip us of our systems of security, but we can also do this ourselves. Then an active purgation of ourselves from enslavement takes place. This is what happened to the evangelical widow; she stripped herself of everything she had.

We can also talk about a similar self-entrusting to God of the widow from Zarephath who met with Elijah (cf. 1 Kings 17:8-16). The widow had a small child and there was a famine in her country. The only things left in her supplies were a handful of flour and a few drops of oil. It was under these conditions that Elijah said to her, "Make me a little cake." The comment of the widow, that this was the last handful of flour, changed nothing. Elijah repeated his request, "Make it for me." The woman replied, "Yes, I will do as you ask and then we will starve to death – my child and I." This was really an acceptance of death since there was nothing left to count on, not even this handful of food. This was God, through Elijah, who took from the widow the remaining food that had given her a certain feeling of security. Then she had nothing.

What does God do with such people? The Bible says that afterward the flour increased, so that despite preparing meals, there was always enough. And it was the same with the oil – the widow and her child did not die. God cannot abandon a person who, by totally entrusting himself to Him, frees himself from mammon and cuts himself off from the systems of security that destroy his faith. **God watches with admiration the miracle of human faith, especially trusting,**

childlike faith, which expresses itself in the act of giving up everything. A person with such faith is capable of saying, *My God, if this is Your will, I am even ready to die since I believe that You love me.* **Faith this deep begets saints.**

When Mother Teresa of Calcutta left her convent of sisters of the Loreto Order in India to care for the dying at the temple of the goddess Kali, she obviously had few possessions and little money. However, very quickly, she gave all that she had to the dying. What then? When night came, there remained only one thing: *God, if you wish, then I will die.* In India, in Calcutta, no one would help her since people there look with indifference upon dying people. In the context of the Hindu religion and the law of Karma, this state of affairs is considered almost normal. A person of Hindu faith would say to you that, since you are dying of starvation, it means that you deserve it. If you die from starvation, you will be reborn into a better existence after death. Mother Teresa of Calcutta understood that she might not find anyone willing to help her. At the same time, however, she believed that God was by her side and that, from then on, she would rely only on Him. There were days and nights when, after giving away everything, Mother Teresa fell asleep in horrible exhaustion. She slept with the certainty that she had nothing for tomorrow – nothing for herself or for the few postulants in the new order and nothing for the mass of dying people who had to be helped. These were lessons of faith and lessons of holiness for Mother Teresa of Calcutta. She had nothing. In these conditions, in the absence of any human systems of security, Mother Teresa of Calcutta emerged as one whom the world looks upon with honor and respect. She is a person who had faith, who believed to the point of folly, who went through difficult lessons to gain faith in situations where humanly speaking there was nothing to rely on. When our whole system of security falls apart, there remains only despair or faith – either terrible despair or heroic faith.

If your faith is not radical enough and if you do not completely trust God's love for you to the point of folly, then you will continue to advance on your way to faith at a snail's pace, or you will go backward. By building a human system of security, you will hinder your growth in faith. Your faith will deepen only when you allow God to be your only support and your only security. **God has the right to request that you give Him everything – everything in the sense of total self-entrusting to Him.**

From the point of view of faith, it is a very good thing that sometimes our support crumbles beneath us because grace is linked to this. You cannot rely on anything but God – not on any of His gifts, nor on any signs of His presence. The Old Testament relates to us that after a terrible defeat of the Israelites by the Philistines that took place during the time of Judges, the Ark of the Covenant got into the hands of the enemy. In the first book of Samuel we read:

> The Philistines then drew up in battle formation against Israel. After a fierce struggle Israel was defeated by the Philistines, who slew about four thousand men on the battlefield. When the troops retired to the camp, the elders of Israel said, "Why has the LORD permitted us to be defeated today by the Philistines? Let us fetch

the ark of the LORD from Shiloh that it may go into battle among us and save us from the grasp of our enemies."

So the people sent to Shiloh and brought from there the ark of the LORD of hosts, who is enthroned upon the cherubim. The two sons of Eli, Hophni and Phinehas, were with the ark of God. When the ark of the LORD arrived in the camp, all Israel shouted so loudly that the earth resounded. The Philistines, hearing the noise of shouting, ... [said], "Woe to us!" (1 Sam 4:2-8).

And the epilogue to this occurrence was:

The Philistines fought and Israel was defeated; every man fled to his own tent. It was a disastrous defeat, in which Israel lost thirty thousand foot soldiers. The ark of God was captured, and Eli's two sons, Hophni and Phinehas, were among the dead (1 Sam 4:10-11).

One may ask why the Israelites suffered such a great defeat. The Ark of the Covenant was a sign of God's presence among them. Therefore, by asking for it to be brought and by placing their hopes for victory in it, they wanted to rely on Him. How should this be understood, that the Israelites, even though they strove to rely on God, suffered such a defeat and that the Ark – the principal sign of God's presence – was taken from them?

This text is very important since it allows us to form a deeper understanding of what it means to rely exclusively on God. The Ark of the Covenant was not God; it was only a sign of His presence. The Israelites had tried to manipulate this principal sign of God for their personal use. The epoch of Judges is a rather depressing time in the history of the Chosen People. We know that a lot of evil things were happening in the lives of the Israelites as well as in the lives of the High Priest. "Now the sons of Eli were wicked; they had respect neither for the LORD" (1 Sam 2:12). In this context the biblical text shows us how the Israelites, not having respect for the Lord, manipulated the sign of God's presence. They felt that after bringing out the Ark of the Covenant victory should take place almost automatically. Faith, however, does not rely on any of God's gifts or any signs of His presence, but only on Him alone – on His power and love. This power and love cannot be manipulated.

A similar thing happened with the temple that was also a principal sign of God's presence for the Chosen People. It was destroyed because it was not meant to be a permanent support for the Chosen People. God called this nation to rely, through faith, solely on Him.

THE ATTITUDE OF ENTRUSTING OURSELVES TO GOD

Christ, who expects us to entrust ourselves to Him, teaches us with His whole life the attitude of total self-entrusting to Him. He came to us as a Child – an Infant who on His own could do absolutely nothing and was totally dependent on the care of adults. Jesus, therefore, from the moment of coming into this world appeared before us stripped of everything. Why did He choose such nakedness? Try to answer this question for yourself.

If Christ had come to earth with His might, if He had annihilated the Roman occupation by force and forced justice upon society, if He had eliminated evil by force, would it have been easier for you to entrust yourself to Him? It is more likely that you would have been afraid of Him, for man is afraid of violence even when used in the name of good – real or alleged. You cannot fear the defenseless Jesus who comes to us in His powerlessness. If you fear God, the mystery of Bethlehem reminds you that **you must not fear God.** He humbled Himself so much, stripped Himself of everything and became so defenseless, to make it easier for you to adhere to Him and entrust yourself to Him. In this way He showed His love that reaches the point of folly. Christ, stripped of everything and poor, wants us to follow Him on the way to our being denuded of human securities. Our true and authentic denudation is our way to imitate Jesus.[8]

In wanting to make Abraham the father of our faith, God had to uproot him. Abraham became a pilgrim, moving about as if in darkness since he did not know where he was going. Leaving his own country and home, he became a naked person – the kind of person who has nothing besides God. Therefore, he depended permanently on God and turned to Him. Freedom from one's own system of security can be attained in a desert, which strips one of everything.

The various human systems of security on which you rely become, in the evangelical definition, mammon. You may believe in it and place all your hopes there, but it is not the real God. **God wants to protect you from false faith in your**

---

[8] Denudation. being stripped of supports and attachments. See Chapter Four, "The Desert" and Chapter Eleven, "Confirmation."–Ed.

life. That is why it is so important to Him that you reject your false god. Everything we place our hope in becomes a god. If you place your hope in a false god, then your hope does not make sense. Whoever has a false god lacks faith, or his faith is very weak and paltry. If in your life there is a false god whom you serve and on whom you depend, then, from necessity, you will come to know bitterness and disappointment. That false master to whom you have entrusted yourself, in whom you have placed your hopes, sooner or later must let you down. Moreover, something in your entrustment to that false master will collapse.

Christ, when saying that you cannot serve two masters, elaborates His thoughts in the form of symbolic images and, through them, teaches us how we should trust – how we should attain that complete entrustment to Him as the true Master. In His Sermon on the Mount, He speaks of the lilies of the field. These flowers are red poppies, the kind that remind us of the poppies of Monte Cassino in Italy. Palestinian poppies and anemones are lilies of the field. What is peculiar to them, apart from their astonishing beauty, is that they are short-lived. This type of flower lives only one day. It is amazing that God creates such a magnificent one-day flower that, as Jesus said, is more magnificent than the greatest splendor of Solomon. How God must care for it, emphasizing all the splendor of beauty in it! This flower belongs to the Lord, just as you do. Speaking about the carefree birds, Jesus appeals to us to be converted and to free ourselves from human tensions, unnecessary worrying, and excessive anxiety (cf. Mt 6:26-34). **We are to be like the lilies of the field and like the birds in the sky, which He, the true Lord Himself, loves and cares for.**

The plea in the Lord's Prayer, "Give us this day our daily bread," is a call to deepen our faith so that God may become our only support. We find here a clear allusion to the situation in the desert that occurred during the exodus of the Chosen People to the Promised Land. Obviously, the desert creates difficult conditions. That is why there were revolts and disobedience. The Lord, however, was ignited with a jealous love, as the Bible states, and took pity on His complaining, sinful people, sending them manna that fell to earth each day. Being in the desert brings forth that which is deeply embedded in man: egoism, mistrust, and the desire to create one's own system of security. Among the Chosen People there appeared a lack of trust in God despite the miracles that were happening. Their greed also surfaced, expressing itself in the need to gather as much manna as possible, even though Moses, in the name of the Lord, warned them, "You may gather enough manna for **today only**." Many, however, did not obey Moses and gathered more. Then the next stage of the miracle took place, but in another dimension. The following day, all the excess – the amount greater than what should have been gathered and was meant to be a system of security – turned rotten and was eaten by maggots (cf. Ex 16:14-21). The Chosen People could not make themselves secure in a human way by accumulating reserves. This was due to the fact that God led them into the desert to strip them of their securities, "Give us **this day** our daily bread." Give us this day – for today, not for tomorrow or for the whole month. We belong to You. You care about what belongs to You. In the desert, the Lord had to fight with human egoism that caused the Chosen People to refuse to trust in Him – even in the face of a miracle. He had to fight for the faith of His people.

Maturity in faith means the willingness to surrender to the Lord everything that He gives us, entrusting ourselves totally to Him. We should not attach ourselves to anything, not to spiritual gifts, and not even to Holy Communion. God's will is the only one reality that we may attach ourselves to without claiming it for ourselves. Everything besides God's will is a gift and a means to reach the goal, but it is not the goal. If we claim the gift for ourselves, God will either destroy it or – through giving us the experience of suffering – show us that we have nothing to offer, that we are helpless, and that it is God who gives us everything.

A truly expressive testimony of St. Leopold Mandic's faith was his gesture of showing empty hands. Those empty hands turned toward God symbolized his expropriation of any gifts – an expression of extraordinary faith. This faith enabled God to perform miracles through him in the confessional. Our gesture of showing empty hands can be directed toward God not only in spiritual matters, as in the case of St. Leopold Mandic, but it can also indicate our attitude of awaiting everything from God. It should accompany us in everything we do in life: in work, in raising our children, in our influence on others, and in prayer. The gesture of empty hands should also accompany us when looking for the greatest of God's gifts to come – the gift of Himself for He is Love that embraces us and in which we are immersed.

ABANDONMENT TO GOD

Your reliance on God by entrusting yourself to Him will not be completely pure unless it takes the form of

abandoning yourself to Him. It could be that you entrust yourself to Him, expecting that He will fulfill your will. If you say, *God, I entrust myself to you, my will be done*, this is still the constant seeking of oneself. Reliance on God has to become the abandoning of oneself to Him. **Lord, let it be as you want** since *You love me and know best what I need and what those whom I love need and what those whom I pray for need*. In our spiritual life and on our way to God, our entrusting of ourselves to Him must become a way of total abandonment to the Lord.

At Christmas in 1887, Celine, the sister of St. Thérèse of the Child Jesus, wanted to give her a joyful surprise. She made a little paper boat and set it on the water. Inside the boat was a small figurine of a sleeping Jesus and on the boat itself was the one word *abandon*.[9] This was the catchword of Thérèse's and Celine's prayer. There were waters on which God would lead them, the waves of life, and they were to abandon themselves to His love.

The theology of spiritual life says that only the abandonment of oneself to God begets internal peace within a person. As long as you do not abandon yourself to the Lord, you will be uneasy, and your heart, filled with unrest, concerns, and problems, will flutter like a moth against a light bulb. **There is no other way to peace than to abandon yourself completely to His will, to His love.**

To St. Gertrude, who was praying for the health of her friend, Christ said, "You interfere, Gertrude, asking for her health since this illness is a great grace, and she is

---

[9] *Story of a Soul: The Autobiography of St. Thérèse of Lisieux*, 3rd. ed., trans. John Clarke (Washington, DC: ICS Publications, 1996), 143.

surrendering to My will and is quickly being sanctified." The French word *abandon* written by Celine for Thérèse on the little boat, has very profound meaning. It means renouncing one's own plans and visions, **leaving everything behind so that one can devote oneself totally to the Lord.** We are so full of our own plans and our own visions; but God's will and God's plans are often different. Then God must foil our plans. **This foiling of our plans is blessed because His love** always wants what is best for us.

A big obstacle that could prevent our abandonment to God can be a **distorted image of God.** This distorted image may be that you see God as a judge, and you are afraid of Him. To fear God, to fear Him who is Love, is terrible. Maybe you are afraid to abandon yourself to Him because you are afraid of what He may do with you. You must remember, however, that this kind of **conscious fear of God hurts His heart deeply.** It is not so with the fear that is instinctive, that arises by itself spontaneously on a psychophysical level, which is really not under your control. However, if on a spiritual level – in your thoughts and in your will – you consciously consent to fearing God, this is a great unfaithfulness. If you fear God, people, or the world in this way, there is no trust in you, nor do you believe in God's embracing love for you.

St. Thérèse of Lisieux briefly said that one has to be like a child and not worry about anything.[10] This one statement contains the whole program of our life: to abandon ourselves to the Lord, that is, not to care about anything because He

---

[10] Cf. "Yellow Notebook," August 6, 1897 in *Thérèse: Last Conversations*, 138.

loves us and takes care of everything. Only then will true peace begin to penetrate our souls and our hearts. We cannot free ourselves from threats that produce fear; but it is very important for us to remove our fear through a conscious act of abandoning ourselves to the Lord.

When St. Paul asked Jesus to remove some kind of great difficulty from his life, Christ answered him that power is made perfect in weakness (cf. 2 Cor 12:8-9). St. Thérèse wrote that **trust and faith are made perfect amidst fears.** So, how great is the role of your fear in God's economy? It is there to provoke an act of faith within you. Fear is a trial of faith, and that is why God allows it, so that you may grow in faith. Trust and faith are made perfect amidst fears.

Fear can contribute to illness in many people. Fear lies at the basis of neuroses and psychoses. **But it can be an outlet to total abandonment to God.** It depends on you. Fear is a challenge issued to you. What will you do with it? Will you allow yourself to be enslaved by its weight? Or will you try to perform acts of abandoning yourself to Him who is infinite power and infinite love. Everything that happens is connected with our decision. We cannot rid ourselves of fear as an emotional state, at least not always. Fear, however, can become a factor that deepens our faith, just as each temptation can.

To St. Margaret Mary Alacoque, the great apostle of the Sacred Heart of Jesus, Jesus said many times, "Leave it to Me to act."[11] Christianity is a religion of grace, a religion that

---

[11] Marguerite Marie Alacoque, *Thoughts and Sayings of St. Margaret Mary: for Every Day of the Year,* complied by The Sisters of the Visitation of Paray-le-Monial, trans. The Sisters of the Visitation of Patridge-Green, Horshan, West Sussex (Rockford, IL.: Tan Books and Publishers, 1986.), 30. (Extracts from vol.3, *Vie et ouevres de Sainte Marguerite Marie,* 1920 ed.).–Ed.

directs us toward allowing Christ to act, toward opening ourselves more and more to His work. What we are called to is the kind of openness that allows Christ to live fully within us. Then He can re-create you into His masterpiece, just as in the case of the Virgin Mary who lived by faith, trust, and complete abandonment to the Lord.

The basic principle of God's action is that **He does not want to impose on you**. If the door to your heart is closed, He will not want to force it open. St. Margaret Mary wrote that Jesus would do everything in her if she only allowed Him to act in her. She said that the Divine Heart of Jesus would desire in her, supply all that she lacked and would love for her.[12] **Abandoning oneself to God is the highest form of self-entrustment to Him, the highest form of reliance on the Lord**. St. Thérèse of the Child Jesus said, "Neither do I desire any longer suffering or death, and still I love them both; it is *love* alone that attracts me...Now, abandonment alone guides me, I have no other compass! I can no longer ask for anything with fervor except the accomplishment of God's will in my soul without any creature being able to set obstacles in the way."[13] Thérèse admits, "It took me a long time before I was established in this degree of abandonment. Now I am there; God has placed me there. He took me into His arms and placed me there."[14] Your self-entrusting to God and accepting His will in everything will be complete if you are able to say, *I love everything you send me*.

---

[12] Ibid., 37.
[13] Thérèse, *Story of a Soul*, 178.
[14] "Yellow Notebook," July 7, 1897 in *Thérèse: Last Conversations*, 77.

THE JEALOUS LOVE OF GOD

God burns with a jealous love for you. It means that **He wants to be your only Lord, your only love** (cf. Ex 30:5; Deut 5:9). He calls us to conversion, which always has two elements: turning "to" and turning "away from." We are to turn away from everything that pushes us away from the only Lord to whom we belong. We are to turn away from our egoism that desires security and is set deeply in our souls. If you have formed some system of security and God has caused your "manna" to rot, then remember, He has done this out of love. **God strips you of that which is your enslavement and which leads to lack of faith in His love.** He is the only Lord, of you and of your "manna," that is to say, the Lord of your daily bread and of your existence. Everything depends on Him. Whether you acknowledge it or not, He remains the only Lord – the Lord who loves you. He does not want you to get lost in the false kingdom of a false god because that kingdom will destroy you. You are His possession – that includes all you own, your body and soul, your work that is dependent on Him, your home that is His, your children who belong to Him, and your time that you often dole out to Him like a miser, despite the fact that all of your time also belongs to Him.

The Gospel says that you cannot serve two masters. The Greek word *douleuein* (to serve) means the type of servitude a slave is engaged in for his master. A slave does not have time for himself. The master controls the slave's time always and completely. **You need to give God everything;** you need to know how to give Him that which is His – this is the program of your conversion. **You must also accept His jealous love**

and accept Him as the only treasure, the only love. The expression "jealous love" contains the entire depth of God's love because He is not jealous for His own advantage, but for yours; He is jealous so that you will not get lost in servitude to false gods.

A person who reaches union with God and attains sanctity is one who has accepted Christ to the very end as the only love. There are two categories of believers: those who collect merits and those who simply try to love. To love not only means to give but, even more so, to accept, to accept the love of another person. To love God is to accept His love – a jealous love for you, a love that is jealous and a folly. This love wants to protect you from everything that threatens your freedom and your faith.

The Lord burns with a jealous love for you. This love is God's torment; it is God's hunger for you, you who are His child, His possession. He will fight for you. His jealous love will at times be difficult, because you sometimes slip through His fingers and walk toward the edge of the precipice, often without realizing it. Therefore, sometimes God will have to shake you; he will have to give you "difficult" graces, but that is in order to rescue you, so that in the end you may entrust yourself to Him – to the jealous love of God.

CHAPTER FOUR

FAITH AS ACKNOWLEDGING ONE'S OWN HELPLESSNESS AND AWAITING EVERYTHING FROM GOD

In the light of faith we can see our own helplessness and await everything from God. Walter Kasper writes that, according to the synoptic Gospels, the meaning of faith is to know one's own helplessness and to trust in the power of God acting through Jesus.[15] A believer does not wait for anything from himself, but awaits everything from the Lord. It is only when we acknowledge our own helplessness in the spirit of faith that we become poor in spirit and allow the power of God to act within us.

---

[15] Walter Kasper, An Introduction to Christian Faith (New York: Paulist Press, 1980), 80.—Ed.

Evangelical morality is not just the morality of the Decalogue, although that is its premise, but it is primarily the **morality of the Beatitudes**, especially the morality of the first Beatitude, "Blessed are the poor in spirit, / for theirs is the kingdom of heaven" (Mt 5:3). They are blessed because it is they, the poor, who actually enter the Kingdom.

"BLESSED ARE THE POOR IN SPIRIT"

He who above all seeks the kingdom of heaven, and therefore seeks sanctity, will find it and find everything else – all the spiritual and temporal gifts necessary for life. "Blessed are the poor in spirit" (Mt 5:3). They are attached to nothing, have nothing, and await everything from God. They are blessed because there is room in their hearts for the Lord. The kingdom of heaven belongs to them because they have God. This is a joyous Gospel about blessed people whose hearts are free for the Lord.

You have faith to the extent of your being poor in spirit. The word "poor" in the biblical sense does not necessarily mean poverty in the material sense. For example, King David, a man at the top of the social scale, was poor in spirit. A person poor in spirit is one who is stripped of self-confidence. He is one who knows that he cannot count on himself or on his own strength. This kind of person is oriented toward awaiting everything from God and is not rooted in temporal things.

If you feel that you are strong in the sense that you possess natural abilities, your faith cannot develop and deepen. That is why you have to experience your weakness;

you have to realize that there are things you cannot do. This will be the call to faith. Your weakness, inability, and helplessness will become a crack through which the grace of faith will squeeze into your heart. **Through your woundedness, God gives you the grace of deepening your faith.** Charles Péguy, a great convert, writes:

> One has encountered an incredible generosity of grace and some unbelievable graces penetrating an evil and even depraved soul, and one has seen as saved that which appeared lost. However, one has not encountered what was varnished to be saturated, what was waterproof to be permeated, and what was hardened to be softened.
>
> From this source derive so many obstacles to the efficacy of grace – grace that, while bringing so many victories in the souls of great sinners, remains ineffective within righteous people.

This is because these "righteous" people, those mature in the evangelical sense, have no deficiencies; they are not wounded. They are powerful, strong, self-sufficient, and mature. Péguy continues:

> Their moral skin constantly intact becomes their shell and armor of faultlessness. They do not present an opening caused by some kind of terrible wound, caused by an unforgotten distress, an inability to overcome regret, a stitch improperly joined, a mortal fear, an invisible and hidden anxiety, a secret bitterness, a fall perpetually masked, a scar badly healed. They do not present this point of entry to grace which, essentially, sin

is. Since they are not wounded, they are not vulnerable. Since they lack nothing, nothing is given to them.

Lacking nothing, they are not given that which is everything. **God's charity by itself cannot heal those who have no wounds.** It is because a man lay on the ground that a Samaritan picked him up...Therefore, the one who has not fallen will not be picked up and the one who is not dirty will not be wiped clean. (Editor translation of *Note conjointe sur M.Descartes et la philosophie cartésienne,* [Joint Note on Descartes and Cartesian philosophy, 1914].–bold emphasis added by author)

The so-called self-righteous adults are impenetrable to grace.

Perhaps in your life there is a terrible unhealed wound, maybe an unforgotten torment, a resentment that you have not been able to get over, some kind of hidden bitterness that accompanies so many things in this life, maybe some kind of disaster. You then think that this is the end, but this is not so. These can be your channel for grace. **God must allow so many wounds, so many hard moments, so that you feel weak and, through this, open to grace.** When you feel very painfully touched, remember that this is a blessed pain that makes room for grace to penetrate your armor of maturity and self-righteousness. All of this is a chance for you to deepen your faith. Through faith your weakness lets the might of God dwell in you. When coming closer to you, God must make you weaker so that you will need Him – so that, as your faith and trust in Him increase, you will seek support from Him. You have to be humbled because you are too great – and wounding humbles. Hence, every wounding gives you a chance to become more and more like an evangelical child. **Sometimes it will take many wounds to become a child so that you will walk "the little way."**

THE MIGHT OF GOD NEEDS THE WEAKNESS OF MAN

God, getting closer to man, weakens him. He does just the opposite of what we would expect. You may believe that it is you who are approaching Him, and that, under those conditions, you should become increasingly stronger and increasingly more able to get along by yourself. However, it is He who is coming closer to you, and His approach makes you weaker – physically, mentally, or spiritually. He does this in order to dwell in you with His might, **since it is your weakness that makes room for His might.** When you are weak, you cannot trust in yourself; you cannot believe in yourself; and then the opportunity comes for you to turn to Him and to desire to rely on Him. So often you shield yourself against this greatest grace, **the grace of weakness**, but St. Paul has already written, "'For power is made perfect in weakness.' I will rather boast most gladly of my weaknesses, in order that the power of Christ may dwell with me...for when I am weak, then I am strong" (2 Cor 12:9-10). **Your own power and strength must collapse sooner or later.** Strictly speaking, there is nothing you can call exclusively your own strength. Any kind of strength is a gift – a gift that you usually claim as your own, and that is why it must be taken from you.

Often St. Maximillian Kolbe felt completely helpless during his unusual apostolic journeys. Frequently the climate was not suitable for his ailing lungs. His body did not tolerate the humidity and the tedious journeys across the sea. These made it difficult for him to breathe. All of this, however, did not stop him from proclaiming the kingdom of the Immaculate, even though it seemed as if he would not survive another hour on the ship. Maybe at that time he spoke to Mary saying, *I cannot last another hour. How then shall I expand your kingdom?* However, this weakness was his whole strength.

If God chooses to act through you, then it will be based on your weakness. If you try to be powerful and forceful in your apostolate, you become an anti-sign. **People do not want your power, your personal power**, since this is demeaning to them. God, in order to make you His sign and to act through you, also does not need your power. The very opposite is the case. He needs your weakness. This idea was very clearly expressed in the Old Testament with Gideon as an example (cf. Jgs 7:1-8, 10). Gideon's enemy had one hundred and thirty-five thousand soldiers, and Gideon had thirty-two thousand, four times less. However, in history there have been victories despite such a disproportion. For God, even this disproportion was too small. He told Gideon to reduce the number of his warriors. The first trial depended on reducing the army from thirty-two thousand to ten thousand. At that point, Gideon's army was thirteen times smaller. In the history of military strategy, victories do not happen with this kind of disproportion; however, man could still claim this as his own and attribute it to his own genius. Therefore, Gideon was still too strong and could count on his own abilities. So God tried him once again; He told him to reduce those ten thousand men to three hundred. At that moment, it was not clear whether the situation was dramatic or comical. It would be really ludicrous to go against the enemy with such a number, when they were four hundred and fifty times stronger. Under those circumstances, only God could be victorious, not Gideon. And Gideon marched with this handful of men and was victorious. This disheartening disproportion would not allow even the temptation for Gideon to claim it as his own. The whole situation was so absurd that it was as though God were smiling and saying, *You see, Gideon, you wanted to be victorious relying on your own abilities and the strength of your armies. Look, you are left with three hundred men against one hundred and thirty-five thousand of the enemy. What can you say to that?* Gideon trusted the Lord and was victorious; he had a victory the likes of which had never before been seen in history.

The Lord places His gift in a fragile, clay vessel **so that whatever we do comes from the power of God, not from us** (cf. 2 Cor 4:7). God stripped Gideon of his human power – made him small and weak; He did something that, in human terms, seems absurd. Something like this can happen in your life. If there is within you thirty-two thousand elements of human power, God will make it ten thousand and then three hundred. You will then be truly weak, almost defeated; and being weak is how you will be victorious. These will be victories, not through your power, but through the might of God.

THE POVERTY OF CHRIST

Faith, as expressed in poverty of spirit, has its example in the life and person of Jesus. To be poor means to be dependent. In the life of Jesus we see three moments when His poverty became extreme. **God became entirely dependent and showed Himself in his powerlessness, as if in defeat, in these moments: Bethlehem, Calvary, and the Most Blessed Sacrament.** If poverty means dependence, then Jesus became completely dependent in **Bethlehem**, where there was a situation of powerlessness – one could even say defeat – because Jesus was not accepted by His own people and had to be born in conditions that were inhumane. Every one of your experiences of powerlessness and the inability to cope with something is partaking in the powerlessness of Jesus.

Terrifying in its expression, **Calvary** is the second situation of the denudation of Jesus. Here He was also unable to do anything to help Himself, since His hands, those hands that had blessed the crowds, were now nailed to the Cross, bleeding. He could not use His feet because those feet, which before had brought love and good news, were now nailed down. Jesus on Calvary was stripped of everything. **The Cross is an expression of the folly of God's love. Here the nakedness of Jesus was extreme.**

Yet another expression of the nakedness of Jesus is the **Most Blessed Sacrament.** Here there is also a situation of powerlessness and defeat, similar to that on Calvary. But of course, this only seems to be a defeat. Jesus is silent in the Most Blessed Sacrament, even when people pray to Him. In the tabernacle He remains naked to the extent that someone can take Him out and move Him wherever they want; one can accept Him as well as desecrate Him. Therefore, someone can do with Him whatever they want, literally whatever they want. **And this is the amazing mystery of the nakedness and poverty of Christ – His kenosis – His complete offering of Himself to man.**

These three situations – Bethlehem, Calvary, and the Most Blessed Sacrament – are situations in which the love of Jesus really reaches the point of folly by leading Him to extreme poverty. But it is through this folly and this poverty that Jesus brings you your redemption, brings you faith. God's silence, His powerlessness, His "defeat," is a scandal for the world that wants a God full of visible power. The Cross was and continues to be a stumbling block for those who do not believe, but for those who have faith, it is the highest power. Your cross, which is your nakedness and poverty, makes room for grace in you – room for the grace of faith.

TO ACKNOWLEDGE THAT EVERYTHING IS A GIFT

Faith is the acknowledgement of one's own helplessness – the belief that one owns nothing, that everything is a gift. It is the awaiting of all gifts from God. The opposite of such faith is pride. A proud person considers all these gifts as his own and attributes them to himself. He thinks that everything depends on him as if the unceasing gift from God did not exist in his life. Of course, faith is a difficult thing. To live in faith means to be born again, reborn to become poor in spirit and to regain the attitude of a child.

A gift should be accepted with such detachment that at any given moment you could return it. This is an astonishing paradox. We are gifted so that, in accepting God's gifts, we are ready to return them. The gesture of our readiness to return to God a gift we have received is a sign that we have not taken possession of it. It is an expression of acknowledging the truth that we possess nothing. A gift returned to God comes back multiplied. Everything is a gift – your body and soul, wife, husband, children, what you have, and what you do – everything belongs to the Lord. **Are you ready to return each of these gifts at any moment?**

The episode of the rich young man, who walked away sadly when the Lord suggested that he should give up material wealth, has its epilogue. After he left, Jesus talked about those who trust in their riches and said, "Children, how hard it is to enter the kingdom of God!" (Mk 10:24). Note that this young man had fulfilled all the commandments. It appears from this that **it is not enough to fulfill the commandments**. It is about him and others like him that Jesus said, "It is easier for a camel to pass through [the] eye of [a] needle than for one who is rich to enter the kingdom of God" (Mk 10:25). It is a statement so strong that the apostles, terrified by this, asked, "Then who can be saved?" (Mk 10:26).

That young man, who appeared to be open to God, was a slave to the worldly life – a slave to his own riches and to social status. St. Luke speaks of him as an official, therefore we know that he held an important position (cf. Lk 18:18). All of this can come between a person and God, and it can become such a great obstacle that, for a person like the young man, it may be very difficult to be saved. Attachment to temporal reality – to what God has created, to that which is only a gift and is not God Himself – can, through enslavement, not only hinder but also make our salvation impossible.

During my journey to San Giovanni Rotondo to see Father Pio, I met a scientist who had also traveled there in order to ask Father Pio to bless his work. He came with two volumes of a published work that he called his *opus vitae* (life's work). During confession, he presented them to Father Pio and asked for his blessing. Father Pio's reaction was frightening. First and foremost, he expressed his astonishment, "This is your *opus vitae*? This is your life's work?" He took the two volumes into his hands and repeated, "Is this your *opus vitae*? Does it mean that you have lived these sixty years to write these two books?" He almost shouted, "Is this *opus vitae*? Is this what you have lived for? And where is your faith?" Then he softened as if he had seen the naïveté of this man and with the gentleness of a father, he asked, "I'm sure you put a great deal of effort into it, didn't you? I'm sure there were a lot of sleepless nights. And how is your health? Well, yes, your heart attack. All this in the name of ambition, to create this type of *opus vitae*?" Padre Pio continued, "See what idols and attachments mean. If you had done the same, but for God, everything would be different. You claimed everything as your own, that this was **your** *opus vitae*, **your** own work." The end of this confession was also in Father Pio's style. He raised his voice again, "If this is all you came with, *va via*, please leave." Father Pio was *brusco* as the Italians say, which means harsh, but behind this harshness laid a great love for each person and each penitent. This was a man who loved, and love is powerful. It was Father Pio's love that was the reason for this shocking conversation and, together with confession, became the real turning point in the life of this scientist who then really started to think differently and look at the world differently.

Abraham, the father of our faith, received a miraculous gift when he was very old: a son was born to him. This was the greatest joy for him, to receive one of the greatest gifts in human terms: a son, an heir. Parents usually claim children for themselves and maybe Abraham succumbed to this temptation. However, when God told Abraham that He wanted him to sacrifice his son, Abraham agreed. He also agreed to give up the gift he had received in a way that was most traumatic for him. What would have happened if Abraham had not wanted to give up his son, if he had rebelled and held fast to the belief that God's request was too cruel? What would have happened then? Isaac would have had to die! The circumstances of his death would have been unimportant. Whether it was because of sickness, or during a battle, or being devoured by a wild animal, he would have had to be taken away from Abraham because he would have stood between Abraham and God. Isaac would have then become an obstacle preventing Abraham's total devotion to God in faith. Not giving up his son would have meant that Abraham claimed him for himself. Taking possession of a gift means destroying it as if it were a blow aimed at oneself and at the gift itself. Abraham, in giving up his son, not only regained him, but more than that, received a gift multiplied – the grace of sanctity in which his son also shared. Abraham and Isaac were the first Holy Patriarchs of the Old Covenant.

THE SEEDS OF DISTRUST

When we analyze the mechanism of how evil is begotten in humankind, we notice that the foundation of evil lies in a lack of simplicity and a lack of childlike trust in God. This is how it has been from the beginning of the history of humankind, from the moment when our first parents Adam and Eve were placed in a situation that tried their faith. At the origin of human history lies the trial of trust. It is as if God posed the question, *Do you trust Me? Do you have the simplicity and trust of a child toward Me?* The Bible clearly states that the first human was attacked by Satan in this very way. Satan did not tempt the first parents to evil, as such. He did not tempt them directly to sin. What he did was to sow distrust in a psychologically perfect way, as only he could do. He did not say, "Be unfaithful; be disobedient." No, he tried to convince our first parents that there is no love, sincerity, or truth in God. At the foundation of the mechanism of evil in Original Sin lies the distrust that was sown, which caused a great psychological resonance. A person who does not trust begins to feel threatened. A person whom I do not trust becomes a threat to me, and I begin to fear him. The sin of distrust brings threat and fear. This fear, which is spoken about at great length in psychology and psychiatry, very often becomes the source of human suffering.

If we are not free from sin, then we cannot be free from that which stems from it: anxiety, fear, and the feeling of being threatened. We are also tempted by these seeds of distrust. If this distrust is toward God, then we feel as if we are locked in a cage, and life in a "cage of threat" becomes something terrible. A person is destroyed by sin also on account of the fear that accompanies sin. The feeling of being threatened becomes the final blow to us since one of the most basic emotional needs for a person is the need for security. From this we can conclude that the fear we do not fight against is our fault.

The redeeming works of Christ continue. Through faith we are incorporated into Redemption, which includes not only our sin but everything that pertains to it. Therefore fear, as well as the feeling of being threatened, become a part of the Redemption. Jesus, dying on the Cross, redeemed us from fear and from the feeling of being threatened, just as He redeemed us from sin. All our lives should be oriented toward an increasingly greater openness toward the redeeming action of Christ. Grace flows continuously from the Cross so that we may be saved from sin as well as from fear.

How are you to fight this fear that surrounds you? If you fight it directly, it will end in a fiasco. There is only one unfailing way: **open yourself up to the redeeming action of Christ through faith like that of an evangelical child.** You must believe that Jesus redeemed you from everything that threatens you, that you are truly free. You should say to yourself: *There is no threat since He has redeemed me and has freed me from everything. I need only to accept this.* **Faith is acceptance – the process of accepting the redeeming action of Christ.**

When Peter was going through one of the gates of the temple, he met a crippled man who begged him for alms. Peter then said to him, "I have neither silver nor gold, but what I do have I give you: in the name of Jesus Christ the Nazorean, [rise and] walk" (Acts 3:6). And the crippled man rose. This begging, crippled man was helpless, and he expected a great deal. He also must have had a lot of childlike faith, for he received more than he expected. You who are crippled by fear, by a sense of being threatened, do not necessarily have to be healed as immediately as that crippled man. It will depend on the degree of your faith, on whether you really have the faith of a child. You can be healed instantly or healed gradually. Just as the crippled man, who symbolizes your situation, was lifted by the hand of Christ, you will be lifted gradually ever higher, and in this way, you will slowly begin to rise. Your gradual lifting is also a redeeming action of Christ.

It is difficult to believe, but it is even harder not to believe. Try to realize as often as possible that you are not alone. Christ, who has redeemed you, is with you. With a childlike feeling of your own helplessness, try to oppose those fears that depress you. Say to Jesus, *I know that you want to cleanse me from this leprosy; I know that You have already redeemed me from it.* Do you know that you could be the witness to a miracle? Christ said, "If you have faith the size of a mustard seed, you would say to [this] mulberry tree, 'Be uprooted and planted in the sea,' and it would obey you" (Lk 17:6). Then you would see that the unlimited power of God is in faith, which in the eyes of the world is such a small "nothing" – just like a mustard seed, the smallest of seeds. You would see that faith opens you to the redeeming works of Christ and, in a miraculous way, removes fear. Then, suddenly, you would feel that you are a free person.

You are called to freedom and peace through faith that opens you to Christ's Redemption. Therefore, you must continually be converted to this faith because faith is a continuous process. This process deepens itself through continuing acts of faith, arising most often in the face of a threat. **Then in every situation, by stirring acts of faith within yourself, you will entrust yourself like a child into the arms of the loving Father.**

The essence of the "little way" of St. Thérèse of the Child Jesus is found in the attitude of a child free from all fear thanks to **childlike trust**. At the origin of mankind, sin arose because of the sowing of distrust. The "little way," which emphasizes the importance of trust and childlike faith in God, is both an antidote to distrust and an exact antithesis of that event. The program of the "little way" strikes at the very root of evil that is caused by lack of trust. The lack of trust, the sowing of seeds of distrust toward God is, in large measure, the source of all of your sins and of all of your existential and psychological anguish, and indirectly, also the source of your physical problems. **If you trust in the Lord, you will sever the root of that which destroys you.** Believe that He loves you. The trial of faith for Adam and Eve was not that difficult, but the Bible speaks also of the terrible trial that God gave to Abraham. He received the terrifying order to kill his own son. It would have been so easy at that time for Abraham to accept the seeds of distrust – not to trust but to rebel. Abraham, however, despite the darkness that surrounded him, trusted. How important is this complete trust in God, the childlike trust in Him, whom we wound most deeply with our sin of distrust.

If you have ever been in a situation when someone whom you loved very much lost trust in you, then you know how painful this is. Yet we are not dealing with an ordinary situation of human friendship injured by distrust; this is a situation of a human distrusting the infinite love of God. How great must be the pain inflicted on this Love by our lack of trust. The words, *I am afraid to turn everything over to God,* hurt like a slap in the face because they are as if you were saying to God, *I don't trust You; I do not know what You are going to do to me.* If a small child were to say this to his mother, it would be extremely painful for her. How great must be the pain that God experiences when man slaps Him with such lack of faith! **Distrust,** in a certain way, is worse than sin **because it is the root and the source of sin.** If you do not want to trust, if your Enemy is able to engraft distrust in your heart, then consequences will have to follow – fear, the feeling of being threatened, and the suffering associated with it Only through the consequences of this evil will you see how far you have strayed. Suffering, fear, and the feeling of being threatened are an incessant call for you to be converted. You will continue to carry the burden of fear until you are converted, until you become like a child who simply entrusts himself into his loving Father's arms. "A patient should be treated for as long as it takes until he learns to pray," wrote L. Szondi. This does not refer to repeating simple prayers. It refers to an attitude of deep prayer, **the trusting prayer of a child who surrenders himself fully into the arms of the Father.**

SPIRITUAL POVERTY AS A CHILDLIKE ATTITUDE

Faith, as the acknowledgement of one's own helplessness and the awaiting of everything from God, **means having a childlike attitude.** A child fully acknowledges that he has nothing, that he is unable to do anything. He is filled with expectations and faith that everything he needs he will receive: the Lord said, "Unless you turn and become like children, you will not enter the kingdom of heaven" (Mt 18:3). Conversion to a childlike attitude is an imperative condition for entering the kingdom of God. At some point in time you must become like a child: trusting, humble, awaiting everything from the Lord. If you do not become like a child here on earth, then this will have to happen in purgatory. The state of being childlike is absolutely imperative, not only for sanctity, but also for redemption.

The evangelical child awaits everything from God, literally everything. The childlike dimension of our faith means not depending on ordinary human calculations, but rather, the stirring of a hunger for something that a child would call a surprise. It is being hungry for a miracle. Your spirit is young only as far as you remain childlike. A person can be very old at the age of twenty. On the other hand, one can be eighty years old and remain young thanks to one's childlike spirit. God is always young, and the Church instituted by Christ is always young; that is why She needs the young in spirit. The Church needs within you the childlike attitude that is able to believe everything. An **"old" person** – someone who relies on his own calculations, who lists pros and cons – **limits the possibility for God to act and sets limits on His love and mercy.** Constantly calculating and predicting if one will be successful or not is a trait of old age. A child grasps for the moon and believes that he will get it – and God wants to give you more than the moon. He wants to give you His kingdom, but if you do not become a child, His hands will be tied.

Children are also the typical evangelical violent ones who Jesus speaks about, who are taking the heavenly kingdom by force (cf. Mt 11:12). When a child wants to get into his home, then he just has to get in. He will continue pounding with his fists or kicking with his feet until he is let in. Jesus said, "Knock and the door will be opened to you" (Lk 11:9). If we knew how to knock at the doors that are closed before us, pounding to get in the way children do, then the doors would have to be opened. **God needs your childlike faith in order to perform miracles in you and through you, since nothing is impossible for God.** "Everything is possible to one who has faith" (Mk 9:23); everything is possible for one who is an evangelical child.

The Gospel tells us of two annunciations: the annunciation to Zechariah and the Annunciation to Mary. Zechariah showed himself to be a man who was old, not only in age, but also in spirit; a person who tied God's hands because he was unable to believe in miracles. In order for him to believe, he had to be touched with a different miracle, which was painful for him, the taking away of his ability to speak. This kind of spiritual old age in a person who is unable to believe in a miracle is something terrible for God. A person lacking the attitude of a child usually negates, as if in advance, the efficacy of his prayers, since within him there is something of Zechariah's attitude. This "righteous before God," faultless old man had no heir and asked for a child. He prayed but, actually at the same time, did not believe that God would listen to him. When the angel announced to him, "Your prayer has been heard. Your wife Elizabeth will bear you a son" (Lk 1:13), it seemed that he did not want to accept this son, did not believe this miracle. All this time he had prayed for a son and, when God heard him, he did not believe it. He raised an argument against his own prayer, "For I am an old man, and my wife is advanced in years" (Lk 1:18). He was an "old" man, no longer believing the Lord. We often resemble Zechariah. Referring to a certain priest, Alessandro Pronzato relates how he called the parishioners to pray for rain and then severely reprimanded them saying, "You came to ask for rain; where then are your umbrellas?"

The second annunciation is the Annunciation to Mary who was so much a child that she was ready to accept everything. Mary was so much at His disposal that God could have "conjured up" extraordinary things for her. She would have accepted everything, believed everything, **since her attitude toward God was permeated with the true power of a childlike spirit**. Do you sometimes think that it is the children and not the old people who rule the world? Yes, children rule the world because a person who has a **childlike spirit has "power over God." God cannot resist a child**; He also cannot deny the eyes of a child filled with true faith and trust.

Peter, while walking toward Christ on the water stopped being a child at a certain point. He started to analyze the situation: *I've walked so far because the water was so smooth, but here comes a wave. Can I go on?* He started to reason in a purely human way, and his faith vanished. At that moment, Peter stopped being a child; that is why he started sinking. He turned out to be an old man and would remain old for a long time. That is why he later betrayed Jesus. It can be said that you sin because you are "old," since being old in spirit closes you off from grace and ties God's hands. God is young and wants to conjure up the moon for you. Was it not the moon for St. Thérèse of Lisieux when He gave her snow on the day she took her veil? God loves this kind of attitude, the kind that does not see limits, and this is the attitude of a child. He sees no limits on possibilities; he is persevering to the point of folly; he is open to that which is new – a child is able to believe.

God is always young and always amazes man. Experiencing God is experiencing an amazing reality. A person with the attitude of an evangelical child is able to be amazed. This kind of person looking at the world can be amazed by everything that surrounds him. **At the moment that you cease to be a child before the Lord, there will be a crisis in your spiritual life: you will begin to regress; you will stop believing and loving.**

Only two categories of people believe in miracles – saints and children. Actually, this is one category, because saints are children in spirit. **In Jesus Christ, God Himself became a child.** He became a child, not only in Bethlehem, but also on the Cross, completely defenseless and dependent upon people for everything. This God, who became a child, wants our helplessness and weakness to lead us toward the complete abandonment of ourselves to Him. He wants to lead us to a limitless trust in His mercy.

The Parable of the Prodigal Son should really be called the Parable of the Merciful Father. The older son, one of the three characters of the drama, does not arouse good feelings in us toward him; he is jealous and impertinent toward his father. Our sympathy lies with the prodigal son, the one who returned, especially because he is like us. In the figure of the prodigal son, we almost spontaneously find ourselves. However, is his attitude truly evangelical? The Gospel says that the return to his father was a calculated one. He returned with the hope that it would be better with his father, since he knew that his father paid his hired workers more than the master whom he served. "I shall get up and go to my father and I shall say to him, 'Father, I have sinned against heaven and against you. I no longer deserve to be called your son; treat me as you would treat one of your hired workers'" (Lk 15:18-19). The parable about the prodigal son seems unfinished. There is a further episode in the **drama of the prodigal son; the drama caused by the fact that there was more of an attitude of the hired help in him than that of a child.** He wanted to be considered by his father as someone with whom a bargain could be struck, just like those who agreed to a daily wage with the landowner (cf. Mt 20:1-16). If the prodigal son returns not as a child but as a hired worker, then he will certainly leave again for a second, a third…or many more times.

The son who has the soul of a hired worker cannot be amazed by love. **The prodigal son did not perceive the wounding of his father nor see the father's pain; he saw only his own misfortune** and sought a way out of it. In the parable of the hired workers, it was the workers of the last hour who were amazed by the landowner's generosity, not those who had been hired for a certain sum. **Only an evangelical child can be amazed,** since amazement implies two contrasting realities. A child knows that he is such a small "nothing," yet he is constantly being gifted with something great. This great contrast between one's own smallness and being richly gifted gives rise to childlike wonder.

A person becomes a Christian when he becomes a child, **when the folly of God the Father's love begins to amaze him.** We discover here a new aspect of the evangelical child – a certain **identity between a child and a contrite sinner.** What does contrition consist in? Contrition is sorrow, a sorrow in the face of the Cross, when, conscious of your own wretchedness and sinfulness, you look upon the Cross and Jesus' wounds and you try in your soul to kiss those wounds that you have inflicted on Him. That is contrition. There was no such contrition in the prodigal son. **Only when, being contrite, you kiss the wounds of Jesus and believe in His love, do you return to God with the attitude of a child.** Only such a return makes any sense. Never return to God as a hired worker, because then you will betray Him again.

We see true contrition in the sinful woman during her meeting with Jesus in the home of Simon the Pharisee. Her simplicity, spontaneity, and authentic contrition testify about her attitude of an evangelical child. In order to express her contrition to Jesus, she came up to Him not caring what people might think, poured ointment, bathed His feet with her tears, and wiped them with her hair (cf. Lk 7:38). This is the simplicity, spontaneity, and contrition of a sinner who is an evangelical child. Those who truly love God are the **contrite sinners** for whom much is forgiven, and **saints,** since they both have the nature of a child. **They are able to be amazed by the love of God, by the folly of His love for them.** It is not hired workers, but children; it is not those who accumulate approval and try to enter into deals with God, but those who believe in His mercy. Indeed, only a child has such faith!

69

PART TWO

THE DYNAMISM
OF FAITH

F aith, as an expression of our relationship with God, is a dynamic phenomenon resulting from a constant process of change. This process is brought about through God's initiative and our answer, revealing our abandonment to Him. Through difficult situations, God tears down our stability. Through trials of faith and denudations, He challenges the abandonment to Him that we have had until that moment in order to make our trust more dynamic. Difficult situations, internal as well as external, prompt our conversion. They impart dynamism to our reliance on Christ, our dependence on Him for support, our entrusting of ourselves to Him, and our awaiting of everything from God.

Faith can become a buried talent if we do not grow in it, but God will not allow this. He does not want our faith to become static. That is why, in the hope of deepening and imparting dynamism to faith, God allows difficult situations to happen that force us to continually make choices. The dynamism of faith becomes a reality through trials that polarize human attitudes. This leads to either a crisis of faith or to its evident intensification. Our faith is continuously changing. A year ago we believed differently, according to the intensity of our faith, and in a year we will believe still differently. Hence, the very important question arises: Is our faith growing, or is it dwindling? We are not so much faithful, as we are becoming faithful; not so much Christians, as becoming Christians; not so much really living the Gospel, as we are trying to live up to it.

CHAPTER FIVE

CONVERSION AS A DIMENSION OF FAITH

C onversion is a permanent and basic dimension of faith. Conversion prevents our faith from becoming static and enables it to undergo a permanent process of deepening. Conversion, as a dimension of faith, is not as much a single act, as it is a process. It means a change in our way of thinking and the apparent transformation of our inner attitudes. During the process of conversion, we turn away from evil and we turn to God. Turning away from evil means not only turning away from sin alone, but also from its source, which is unruly self-love.

Whenever Jesus reproached His apostles, it was almost always due to their lack of faith. Jesus would often reproach them for not believing or for having too little faith. In this one can perceive an evangelical paradox – it was those who followed Jesus, who believed in Him, that He reproached for their lack of faith, and He did this many times. **The purpose of questioning the apostles' faith was for their conversion.** You have to question your own faith. You have to be convinced that your faith should constantly grow and that its present condition will not suffice. This follows the principle that what you have achieved today will not be sufficient for tomorrow.

A HAPPY FAULT

Our faith should develop through the permanent process of our conversion. Christ's rising from the dead means that there is no ultimate failure in our life, that no life is doomed, and that no evil is final. This is stated in the Offertory of the former Liturgy of the Mass, "God... miraculously created the dignity of human nature and even more miraculously restored it." God would not allow evil if He were not able to extract good from it. Our sin can become the "happy fault" that is mentioned in the Liturgy of Holy Saturday. **God can turn every one of our faults into a *felix culpa* (happy fault).** It is a fault that will remind us and show us, in the light of faith, how much we are loved by the One who died and has risen for us. However, not every fault becomes a happy fault. There are times when you do not return to Christ immediately after the fall, and you may even become more hardened and intractable. It is then that the real tragedy takes place, because in this situation God is unable to forgive you.

All of your sins and infidelities should become happy faults, but this can happen only if you are contrite and you long for forgiveness. That is why God, in His desire to help you and to overcome your obstinacy, always approaches you first so that He may induce you to desire forgiveness.

God, who does not remember the wounds inflicted by us, constantly opens His Heart to man. He does it in many ways. He often reveals Himself to us and calls upon us through the saints, whom He fills with His own Divine love, or through the ministers of the Word and of the sacraments, especially the sacrament of Reconciliation. Father Huvelin, the confessor who led Charles de Foucauld onto the path of conversion, said that he was given the grace of an unusually fervent desire from God to absolve people from their sins. This longing to grant absolution, which God gave to Father Huvelin, revealed God's own constant and insatiable desire to forgive our sins. This is why you should fight with your sadness. If you have strayed from God, regardless of how far you have wandered away, you can always return. **After every fall, remember that He is waiting. When you return and ask His forgiveness, you make Him happy, because you allow Him to love you through forgiveness.**

All your infidelities and sins will become happy faults if they help you know the mercy of the Lord more deeply. They will become happy faults if they make you more trustful and humble – trusting the Lord more and yourself less. You will grow in faith after they have been forgiven.

Your transgressions will become happy faults if knowing that you have hurt Jesus pours new life into your love for Him. They will become happy faults if this knowledge deepens your desire to give yourself over to Him – so that your heart may beat exclusively for Him, just as His wounded Heart beats exclusively for you.

THE CONSEQUENCES OF EVIL

The unusual love that God has toward sinners and God's pedagogy toward us is shown in the parable of the prodigal son. If our faith becomes lukewarm and has no expression, God can allow us to fall. God does not want evil, but He may want its consequences, since the consequences of evil impart grace and the call to be converted. This can be seen very clearly in the example of the prodigal son. In Christ's parable (cf. Lk 15:4-32), there was a father who loved and two sons who did not love. The fact that the elder son did not love is clearly seen at the end of the parable when he showed his impertinence toward his father and jealousy toward his brother. The younger son also did not love his father. He did not leave his father for a short time, but forever. The father did not oppose his son's leaving, although he could have. He let him take his share and leave, for love cannot be forced upon anyone. We know the consequences of the son's leaving his father's house. We know that he sank lower into decline and that life was increasingly more difficult for him.

In our commentary, we can try to find certain elements that were not directly revealed in the parable. We can, for example, assume that the father found out through his servants what was going on with his youngest son – that he was starving, had nowhere to live, and was a downtrodden tramp. Let us assume that the father, forthrightly or secretively, could have sent a servant to his son with a bag of money wanting to save him from this kind of downtrodden life. This would have given the son the possibility of living a normal life or of living a life of debauchery. Would this type of constant help from the father have caused the son to return someday? Everything seems to indicate that it would not have. That means that a father who loves his son should not shield him from the evil consequences of his own deeds despite the pain felt in the father's heart.

As a consequence of the evil committed by the prodigal son, two people were "crucified": the father, because of the pain he felt over his son's life of misery and failure, as well as the son himself, as a result of his own failures. A father who loves his son should wait, however, until the evil is fulfilled and the consequences begin to take effect, even if there is risk involved. These consequences of sin were what wounded the son's self-love and inclined him to come back. We know that the time came when the measure of evil was full, when the downfall of the son was not only a moral failure in all its depth, but it also brought the ultimate disgrace. He wanted to fill his stomach with husks that were for the pigs, and pigs were considered unclean animals by the Palestinians. Therefore, this was symbolic of hitting the very bottom; it could not have been worse. And then the consequences of evil began to take effect. It was so bad for the son that he had a calculated, cold thought that it would be worth his while to return to his father, because his father treated his servants and hired workers better than the master for whom he was working. It was not love for his father that decided the return of the prodigal son, but simply mercenary self-love, a cold calculation that it would be better for him – **not for the father, but better for himself**.

Upon returning, he saw his father running out to meet him; he found himself in his father's arms and saw tears of joy in his father's eyes. Then he was clothed in the finest robe, received a ring, and saw that his father was preparing a feast for him. **Only then was there a chance that the son would discover his father's love.** This is how the consequences of evil may be connected with grace. God may want them so that they lead us to conversion. Sometimes only a failure and the suffering it entails are able to shock us and lead to our conversion. Conversion requires contrition of heart and longing for forgiveness. God, who wants us to achieve contrition and longing, runs out to meet us first. In His desire to forgive, He lowers Himself so drastically that, as saints say, He sometimes becomes as if a beggar calling out for help.

The scene of the suicide of assistant commissioner Scobie, the main character in Graham Greene's book, *The Heart of the Matter*,[16] is shocking. In the last moments of his life, after he had taken a lethal dose of pills, the dying commissioner seems to hear that "Someone" is desperately searching for him and calling him. He hears calls for help, a cry of distress, groans of pain. Responding to this call, Scobie manages to drag back, through infinite distance, his remaining consciousness to give an answer that will save him, "Good God, I love…"

Roles seem to be paradoxically changed. It is not Scobie who is asking for help. It is God, who has identified Himself with the wretched man, who calls out for help…for Himself. In the last moment of Scobie's life, God calls out to Him, *Help me forgive you, allow me to save you!*

---

[16] Graham Greene, *The Heart of the Matter* (New York: Viking Press, 1948), 229.

WE CANNOT KNOW CHRIST IF WE DO NOT KNOW OURSELVES

We have to first admit to our sin for it to become a happy fault. In his Gospel, St. John tells us about Christ's promise that when the Holy Spirit comes, the Consoler, He will convince the world about sin (cf. Jn16:8). Therefore, one of the functions of the Holy Spirit, who descends on the world, **is to convince us of our sin.** This is the initial grace, fundamental to our interior life, which is granted to us by the Holy Spirit so that we can be convinced of the fact that we are sinners.

It is not enough, however, for us to accept this first grace of the Holy Spirit. If we were to know only the reality of our sin, it could ruin us. Our lives would become completely weighed down by our own evil; our lives would be marked with restlessness, stress, and sorrow. There has to be an opening within us for a further gift of the Spirit, for the **discovery through faith of God's love for us.**

Pope John Paul II, during his homily on June 2, 1979, at Plac Zwyciestwa (Victory Square) in Warsaw, said these memorable words, "A man cannot be completely understood without Christ. Or rather, a man cannot understand himself completely without Christ." This means that, if we do not take into consideration that Christ has entered into our lives, our perception of ourselves is reduced and, therefore, is false. If the Holy Spirit shows us that we are sinners, but we do not discover Christ who loves us, then we could break down. Certain relationships are so important to man that they seem to belong to his essence. Love is one of these relationships.

We cannot come to know ourselves without Christ, because **without Christ we cannot come to know that we are loved,** that we have been redeemed and chosen. By the fact of being chosen, this love becomes an integral part of our "self," and we cannot fight against it.

There is a second part to the truth spoken of above: **we cannot know Christ without coming to know ourselves.** We cannot comprehend who God is, we cannot believe in His greatness and His love for us, if we do not first uncover the truth about ourselves. If Christ loved you because you were worthy of love, it would not be meaningful. A person, even one without faith, is able to love someone who is worthy. Christ's love, as God's *agape*, is love that comes down from on high and loves that which is unworthy so that it may become worthy. **The more clearly you see your sinfulness, the more honestly you admit to it, the more you will rediscover Christ and fully believe in Him.** This is the paradox of faith: we cannot know Christ without coming to know ourselves. That is why it can be said that only the saints really know Christ because they have come to know themselves thoroughly and have seen the enormity of their own sinfulness. This has allowed them to discover the folly of God's love, which they have sometimes expressed in their prayers by saying, *Lord, it is a folly that you love me so much – me, such a great sinner!* **The moment of astonishment,** the characteristic trait seen in every authentic religious experience, can be seen here. A person who recognizes that he is a sinner and believes in God's love starts to see that God is truly "crazy" in His love for him.

IN THE FACE OF ONE'S OWN EVIL

The fight for faith as the process of conversion entails overcoming haste, restlessness, stress, and especially sadness. **Sadness is an evident indication of self-love severing the very roots of faith, the roots of abandonment to God.** This concerns sadness that appears in situations of temporal difficulties – when something is taken away from us or we lose something. But even more so, it concerns the sadness that comes about in the face of spiritual difficulties – when we fail, when we are unfaithful. Sorrow has a paralyzing effect on our faith. After a fall we should not feel down in spirit since we hurt God more in this way than by the sin itself. Moreover, saints say **that after a fall we are to await graces greater than before the fall.**

The battle to accept defeats and failures in our lives should include even the smallest matters. When playing chess with his brothers, St. Maximillian genuinely liked to lose. He turned away from self-love so that he could fully turn toward the Lord.

In the light of faith, try to look at your own imperfections in such a way that you are not saddened by them: Christ accepts you as you are. You can go to Him with all your imperfections and weaknesses. He will repair what you have done wrong and complete all that you lack.

Here you face an unusually important dilemma. On the one hand, you are to reject the evil that is within you, and on the other hand, you are to accept yourself. You cannot love your imperfection itself, yet you can want only its consequences. The only purpose of this imperfection is so that you can become ever more humble, trusting, and faithful. The fact that you sin should not surprise you. Rather, in the spirit of humbleness, you should be surprised when you don't fall. If you are surprised or discouraged because of falls, then that means you have trusted in your own strength instead of allowing yourself to be carried in Jesus' arms. "But in one act of love, even *unfelt* love, all is repaired,"[17] Thérèse of the Child Jesus wrote to her sister Celine. One should not "become discouraged over one's faults," said the Saint, "for children fall often, but they are too little to hurt themselves very much."[18] Thérèse of Lisieux truly liked to entrust her faults and infidelities to Jesus. She said that, in this way, she wanted to attract His mercy, since He came to sinners and not to the righteous. How important all this is to us who are saddened by our falls.

"What does it matter, my Jesus, if I fall at each moment," wrote St. Thérèse. "I see my weakness through this and this is a great gain for me... *You can see* through this what I can do and now You will be more tempted to carry me in Your arms."[19] As we approach our goal, which is God, He seems to get further and further away. This is normal and proper. Thérèse, seeing herself getting increasingly distant from God, was not saddened by this at all. "Oh, how happy I am to see myself imperfect and to have such need of God's mercy at the moment of my death!"[20]

---

[17] Thérèse to Céline, LT 65, October 20, 1888 in *Letters of St. Thérèse of Lisieux: General Correspondence*, vol.1, 1877-1890, trans. John Clarke (Washington DC: ICS, 1982), 467.
[18] "Yellow Notebook," August 6, 1897 in *Thérèse: Last Conversations*, 139.
[19] Thérèse to Céline, LT 89, April 26, 1889 in *Letters of Thérèse*, 1:557.
[20] "Yellow Notebook," July 29, 1897 in *Thérèse: Last Conversations*, 116.

If you feel that you are sinful and weak, you have a special right to Jesus' arms, because He is the Good Shepherd who looks for lost sheep, those who are weak and helpless and who cannot keep up with the flock. Allow Jesus to take you upon His shoulders. Allow Him to love. Believe in His love.

To have the right to rest upon His shoulders you must be humble. You must admit and believe that you are a sinner, weak and helpless. At the same time, you must believe in His love, believe that He takes you upon His shoulders because of the very fact that you are a sinner, weak and helpless. Faith will make you grateful for His never-ending love for you – a sinner, weak and helpless, in the temporal life as well as in the spiritual life.

THE SACRAMENT OF CONVERSION

When you approach the sacrament of Penance, which can be called the sacrament of conversion, with true contrition, your faith always has a great opportunity for growth. The sacrament of Penance often does not perform its true role in your life because it becomes routine and ordinary, with lack of preparation and disposition. You forget that the sacrament of Penance, not only the Eucharist, is a particular channel for grace and a special time for your meeting with Christ. Maybe you also forget to pray for your confessor or spiritual director so that he may also become a more perfect instrument of God and an assistant in the process of your conversion.

Take a deep look within yourself. **Examine your conscience** and see toward what your life is directed, what is most valuable to you, and **who Jesus Christ is to you.**

Primarily, you should confess from this basis: *Who is Jesus Christ to you? What is your fundamental choice? Do you really, ultimately choose Him?* This is where the confession of sins should begin, for this consideration is most important. If you do not choose Christ, then your other sins are the consequences of this fundamental fault.

There can be various kinds of sin. There are sins committed and sins of negligence. And the sins of negligence are the worst. Among these is the sin of abandonment – **you abandon Christ, leave Him and give Him only a small corner in your heart**. This is your greatest evil. This compromise and lack of radicalism shows that Christ does not represent the greatest value in your life, that He is not everything to you, that your faith is always lukewarm.

Of the five conditions of the sacrament of Penance, the most important one is the **act of contrition**. How do you spend your time before confession? It is contrition that should directly prepare you for the meeting with Christ, for it can best open you to this channel of grace, the sacrament of conversion. Maybe you do not fully appreciate that the time you take in preparing for the sacrament of Penance is priceless. This time should be primarily spent on awakening contrition. **Contrition** is your attitude in the face of the Cross, the feeling that you wounded Christ with your sin and that you desire God's forgiveness and the repair of evil. The fruitfulness of the sacrament of Penance depends on your contrition becoming ever deeper. **You cannot be converted until you are truly and fully contrite.**

One could say that two types of religious attitude exist: one of them could be called "egocentric" and the other "theocentric." In the first case, a person focuses on himself. He does not consider God but only his own situation. In order to be right before God, he goes to confession with the thought of cleansing himself, for his sin is a burden. For a person such as this, confession can become his own "aspirin" for a painful conscience, a pill meant to placate himself and to restore his good feelings about himself. This is constant concentration on oneself. This kind of person, having received absolution, leaves the confessional maybe not completely sad, but not happy either. This is because he is still concentrating on the evil of which he has just rid himself.

When we look at Judas' behavior after betraying Jesus, we can discover many elements of confession. There is an examination of conscience because Judas thought about what he had done and realized his own evil. Sorrow appears here as well; Judas was truly sorry. He even wanted to change; hence, he had the intent to make reparation for his sin. There is also a confession of sin. Judas went to the chief priests and said, "I have sinned in betraying innocent blood" (Mt 27:4). He even made satisfaction for his sin when he threw the thirty pieces of silver that he had received from the chief priests back at them. He did not want blood money. Actually, you can see in Judas' behavior and attitude almost everything that takes place in confession. There is only one thing, the most important thing, missing. That is **faith in Jesus' mercy.**[21] That is why Judas' "confession" was so sad, tragic, and ended with despair and suicide.

---

[21] Louis Evely, *Joy*, trans. Brian and Marie-Claude Thompson (New York: Herder & Herder, 1968), 73-74 (bold emphasis added by author).

Our confession should be a confession like Peter's: he believed in the mercy of Christ and concentrated, not as much on his own sin, but on forgiveness. A person with the "theocentric" religious attitude does not dwell very much on his own sin. Through faith he considers sin as an advantage in discovering God's mercy. Going into the confessional, he thinks primarily about the fact that he has hurt Christ and wants to renew a friendship that he has wounded. Through contrition and sorrow, he wants to allow Jesus to forgive him and, through this, to bring him joy: "You crucified Christ," the holy Curé of Ars John Vianney would say; and "when you go to confession, you must understand what you are going to do; it might be said that you are going to un-nail our Lord from his cross."[22]

If you wound Christ, then His wounds bleed. You should therefore take part in the sacrament of Penance so that these wounds can heal. **You should come because of Him – not to pacify yourself, but to invoke His happiness** at shaping within you a new-born person. This is brought about through sacramental graces.

Some feel guilty that they do not improve after confession. Maybe you even think that confession should serve to make you better, and if you do not become better, then you feel that your confession is senseless. Maybe you feel that if you are supposed to be a better person and you do not become one, then it is better not to go to confession because there is no progress. On the other hand, when you yearn to be better, when you are extremely anxious about your progress, it is

---

[22] Daniel Pezeril, *Blessed and Poor: The Spiritual Odyssey of the Curé of Ars*, trans. Panzy Pakenham (New York: Random House, 1961), 196.—Ed.

apparent that you do not really want God. You do not want His mercy as much as your own perfection. Here lies your lack of faith. You go to confession so that eventually you will be so good that you do not need God who is Mercy Himself. You go to God for forgiveness so that you will not need His forgiveness anymore, so that you can go on without Him, even though He always wants to forgive you, to forgive with joy.

How little faith we have in God's desire for continual forgiving. Among those who leave the confessional, there are always so few joyous faces. And yet, after confession, the world should be different for you, brighter, enlightened by faith in the merciful Lord.

In the Gospel, all "confessions" end with a feast. The Lord was a guest at the house of Zacchaeus. Another time the tax collector Matthew, the future Evangelist, invited Christ to a feast. Matthew also invited other tax collectors and sinners so that they could all celebrate with joy that he had received forgiveness. A feast was also prepared by the father of the prodigal son. **The Gospel constantly links forgiveness with joy.**[23]

Contrition is a decisive element in conversion. In the sacrament of Reconciliation you meet with Christ who wants to forgive you and heal the wounds inflicted on you by your sin. However, if you do not show Jesus your wounds, then He cannot heal them.

---

[23] Louis Evely, *Joy*, 92 (bold emphasis added by author).

If your contrition has no bounds, then the mercy of the Lord will also have no bounds. Think what your confessions are like. Contrition is an act of humility. Humility should increasingly grow within you, and hence, contrition should also continually grow. There is never enough contrition and never enough sorrow for the sins committed. The more you consider yourself a sinner and worse than others, the more you make room for grace and for your faith.

The sacrament of Penance should be an awaited sacrament – one should hunger for Christ present in it. This is a special time of your meeting with Christ. Love wants to be hungered for; otherwise, Love is wounded.

THOSE WHO GUIDE YOU TOWARD THE SACRAMENT OF CONVERSION

One of the patrons of the sacrament of conversion is Zacchaeus. When we mention this unusual person, we are reminded, in contrast, of the rich young man in the Gospel. It must have been very difficult for the "righteous" rich young man to be contrite. He had followed all the commandments of the Decalogue, so why should he be contrite? But Jesus said that for such a person it would be very difficult to enter the kingdom of heaven. The rich young man did not see within himself the greatest evil, the fact that he was so attached to riches and position that he did not choose God completely. He felt that since he followed the Decalogue he was "all right" before God. We don't know what happened to him later, but the evident pain felt by Jesus after he left indicates just how bad his spiritual state was.

Next to the "righteous" young man, the Gospel shows us an *extreme* case, the scoundrel Zacchaeus. This harsh description can be used because Zacchaeus, the chief tax collector (meaning he was chief of the collaborationists and thieves) was really a person worthy of pity, in his own opinion and in that of the others around him. When this great sinner saw the merciful look of Jesus, something was touched inside of him, and then his unusual reaction ensued, "Behold, half of my possessions, Lord, I shall give to the poor, and if I have extorted anything from anyone I shall repay it four times over" (Lk 19:8). Who among us would be able to give up half of their possessions to the poor and make amends for wrongs four times over? In this incident there is a folly of generosity by a contrite sinner who discovers that he is loved. **Zacchaeus was truly overcome with astonishment and happiness.** Jesus turned to the "righteous" young man with the encouragement to give up his riches, but He said nothing to Zacchaeus – he did this on his own, without encouragement. Therefore, we have the contrast between a "righteous" man who did not answer the "look of mercy" and sadly walked away and the ringleader of thieves who turned out to be so sensitive to God's love.

The side candelabras found in many Polish churches are called "*zacheuszki*" from the name Zacchaeus. The symbolism is profound. The *zacheuszki* remind us of the unusual incident in which Jesus did not go for a meal with somebody "righteous" such as the rich young man. Instead, He said to the ringleader of thieves, "Zacchaeus, come down quickly, for today I must stay at your house" (Lk 19:5). Coming to someone's house in those days meant entering into a kind of spiritual communion. This was not an ordinary visit for a meal or party. It was not only to eat something, but also to enter into a special, intimate relationship. Jesus chose Zacchaeus to enter into this personal communion with Him. Coming to his house, the house of presumably the most notorious thief in Jericho, He consecrated it just by His presence. Because of this, the house of Zacchaeus became almost a temple or sanctuary. Sometimes, maybe we feel like saying to Jesus, *Lord Jesus, what poor taste You have if You chose the home and heart of a thief as Your sanctuary.* **But that is the way God is – to the point of folly in His love for man.** Jesus came to Zacchaeus to bring redemption to his home. Bringing redemption to his home meant bringing it, not only to Zacchaeus himself and his family, but also to all of those similar to Zacchaeus – tax collectors and sinners – who came to him and sat with him at his table. Jesus came to enter into a communion with them, to receive them into the temple that He consecrated. **Zacchaeus' heart became God's sanctuary, for it was truly contrite.** Only from the heart of the contrite can Jesus make his true sanctuary.

The good thief is also a patron of the sacrament of Reconciliation. His "confession" took place on the cross. There he admitted his guilt, "And indeed, we have been condemned justly, for the sentence we received corresponds to our crimes" (Lk 23:41). What was happening within his soul remains a mystery to us. Only by the results can we try to assume a unique miracle of grace. This man must have been very contrite because with certainty he would have considered himself to be the worst. According to public opinion he was a criminal and a disgraced person since his crucifixion meant also being deprived of all rights. This criminal was dying by torture in public view and accepted this with his statement, "We suffer justly." It is as if he were saying, *Yes, this should happen to me; I deserve this.* Somehow, he must have perceived the depth of his sinfulness and must have brought himself to be profoundly contrite. It is certain that his attitude of contrition and deep humility made his heart ready to accept God's gift of faith. How great must have been his faith if, in the dying Jesus next to him – beaten, spat upon, and still jeered at – he recognized the King, "Jesus, remember me when you come into your kingdom" (Lk 23:42). It is so difficult for us to be converted because there is too little contrition in our hearts. If there is so little contrition, then our faith is very shallow.

CONVERSION TOWARD RADICALISM

The process of your conversion should lead you to evangelical radicalism – the radicalism of faith to which God calls you through the words of St. John in the Book of Revelation: "I wish you were either cold or hot. So, because you are lukewarm, neither hot nor cold, I will spit you out of my mouth" (Rev 3:15-16).

St. John of the Cross stresses the importance of radicalism using an image of two tethered birds.[24] One of them is tied by a cord and the other by a thin thread. In the end, their situation is similar since both birds are tethered. The situation will change only when there are no ties.

---

[24] John of the Cross, *The Ascent of Mount Carmel* in *The Collected Works of St. John of the Cross*, rev. ed. trans. Kieran Kavanaugh and Otilio Rodriguez (Washington, DC: ICS, 1991), 143.

The opposite of radicalism is compromise – compromise in desires, in attitude, in prayer. God is a maximalist. He wants to give you everything, but you keep wanting too little and asking for too little. You still do not seek what is most important, that which would be a realization of your purpose in life: Christ fully living and reigning within you. Do you know how much you tie God's hands when you ask for a little and are content with a compromise? Everything in our lives should be directed toward the one goal **that Christ can grow and reach His full dimension within us**. Everything should work toward this. That is why God requires radicalism in our petitions as well. God may not answer them since we ask for "too little." The fulfillment of our petitions – for a place to live, for good health, and for work – may make us think that we do not need God anymore. If this would not help us to follow the Lord to the end, then God may not want to answer such prayers. In His folly, God wants to give you everything. He wants to give you the kingdom, but you, wanting so little, make it impossible for Him.

Seek first, meaning primarily, the kingdom of God and His righteousness and everything else will be given to you (cf. Mt 6:33). Someone once said that if you do not primarily seek the kingdom of God, then everything else will be taken from you. Every one of your problems and each difficulty is ultimately a call from God for you to desire more, infinitely more. You should seek above all else the kingdom of God since then all else will be given to you. This is a call from God for your conversion, for your faith.

Marie was speaking about the radicalism of her sister, St. Thérèse of the Child Jesus, when she said to Thérèse,

"You are possessed by God."[25] Possessed, in this context, means the desire to give everything to the Lord. Try to follow her example by desiring to give everything, increasingly more, so that evangelical radicalism is embraced by your will – so that you, too, can become "possessed" by God. You can then repeat these words of St. Thérèse, "I *choose all* that You will."[26] In the evening on the day of her death, September 30, 1897, she said, "Never would I have believed it was possible to suffer so much! Never! Never! I cannot explain this except by the ardent desires I have had to save souls."[27] St. Thérèse suffered for you also, so that you, too, could be "possessed" by God like she was – so that you, too, could live an evangelical radicalism as she did.

St. Ambrose emphasizes that God does not look at what we offer to Him as gifts, as much as at what we reserve for ourselves. God is a jealous God. He loves you to the end and wants you to open yourself up fully for His gifts so that He can bestow everything on you. The meeting of Jesus with the rich young man is mentioned three times – in the Gospel of St. Matthew, St. Mark, and St. Luke. This was really an unusual meeting:

> As he was setting out on a journey, a man ran up, knelt down before him, and asked him, "Good teacher, what must I do to inherit eternal life?" (Mk 10:17).

---

[25] Sister Marie of the Sacred Heart to Thérèse, LC 179, September 17, 1896 in *Letters of St. Thérèse of Lisieux: General Correspondence,*, vol. 2, 1890-1897, trans. John Clarke (Washington DC: ICS, 1988), 997.

[26] Thérèse, *Story of a Soul*, 27.

[27] "Yellow Notebook," September 30, 1897 in *Thérèse: Last Conversations*, 205.

Jesus answered him:

> "If you wish to enter into life, keep the
> commandments... 'You shall not kill; you shall
> not commit adultery; you shall not steal; you shall
> not bear false witness; honor your father and your
> mother;' and 'you shall love your neighbor as
> yourself'" (Mt 19:17-20).

The young man said to him:

> "Teacher, all of these I have observed from my
> youth." Jesus, looking at him, loved him and said
> to him, "You are lacking one thing. Go, sell what
> you have, and give to [the] poor and you will have
> treasure in heaven; then come, follow me." At that
> statement his face fell, and he went away sad, for
> he had many possessions (Mk 10:20-22).

Further describing this scene, St. Luke goes on to tell us
something unusual and surprising:

> Jesus looked at him [now sad] and said, "How
> hard it is for those who have wealth to enter the
> kingdom of God!" (Lk 18:24).

The disciples were astonished by these words. We would also
be astonished. He had kept all the commandments. Jesus,
however, "looked at him" and said how difficult it is for a
man like him to enter the kingdom of God. This text is
shocking. As if knowing how difficult this was for them, Jesus
repeated this to the apostles saying:

> "Children, how hard it is to enter the kingdom of
> God!... It is easier for a camel to pass through
> [the] eye of [a] needle than for one who is rich to

enter the kingdom of God." They were exceedingly astonished and said among themselves, "Then who can be saved?" (Mk 10:24-26).

It appears from these words that it is not enough to keep God's commandments, that Christ's **call to folly, which means to evangelical radicalism, is our obligation.** We must, therefore, continually be converted toward this kind of radicalism. St. Teresa of Avila, commenting on this text, said that the rich young man lacked a seed of folly. He was, as St. Luke writes, an official. He therefore had an important position. Thus, he would have had to give up many things, in fact everything. In his situation it would be a folly. He would have had to accept people saying that he had lost his mind, because to give everything up is not that simple. Jesus says, however, that only he who gives up everything for God will enter the kingdom of heaven. It is not enough to love your neighbor as yourself. After all, the rich young man had followed all the commandments.

All of us are called to folly. Without that seed of folly we cannot follow the Lord to the end. Sooner or later we will have to leave everything and detach ourselves from everything. It will be most difficult to leave everything at the end when we are dying. Then we will have to do it, but with great pain, and the Lord wants to save us from this pain. He would like us to leave all our riches now, but not necessarily in the literal sense. It seems astonishing that the Lord demands so much of us, but this demand of God comes from His desire for our freedom and for our own good. Evangelical folly consists in us giving up **everything that is ours for God, and He in turn giving us everything that is**

His. We give up our paltry everything, and He gives us His wonderful everything, His Godly everything. Let us learn from Mary who is the example for us. She truly gave up everything to the Lord and followed Him to the end – the Mother of our abandonment to God, the Mother of our radicalism.

CHAPTER SIX

THE "VIRTUE" OF HUMOR AS A HELP TO FAITH

G od is infinite Mercy. He forgave David his adultery and murder, He forgave the greedy tax collector who was a traitor, and He forgave the criminal on the cross. However, there is something that makes it impossible for God's mercy to be poured out, and something that God detests in you – it is your unwavering, absolute seriousness; it is your belief that you are someone important. Seeing this, it is as though God makes a gesture of spreading out His hands in helplessness. God finds your feeling of importance funny and absurd. "The one enthroned in heaven laughs" (Ps 2:4). If you look at yourself **in the light of faith,** you will see that **all your pretense of absolute seriousness and esteem is truly funny.**

The feeling of self-importance is largely opposed by the "virtue" of humor. It becomes very useful for the growth of

our faith, which is to see the world in the proper light
and with the correct sense of proportion. Humor is seeing
the world on the axis of absurdity and nonsense. We
have a patron of humor, St. Thomas More. We also have a
wealth of literature on this subject by authors such as
G. K. Chesterton, C. S. Lewis, Bruce Marshal, Frank Sheed,
and others. They write about the value of comedy, about
humor being used as a "religious remedy" benefiting faith,
and about the "theology" of humor.

JANSENISM AS A THREAT TO FAITH

The heresy of Jansenism became a great threat to faith in the
seventeenth century. Cornelius Jansen of Louvain taught
that through original sin human nature became completely
corrupt and given as prey to concupiscence; God granted His
graces only to the chosen ones, and all others were destined
for eternal damnation. This pessimistic outlook on human
nature was coupled with the belief that Christ did not die for
all mankind, but only for the chosen ones.

Jansenism set unattainable requirements with regard to
Holy Communion. In order to receive Holy Communion, it
was necessary to have a disposition that the average Christian
usually did not possess. Complete freedom from sin – even
venial sins – and absolute, pure love of God were required.
The Eucharist became a payment for virtue rather than the
nourishment that strengthens faith and love. In the churches
dominated by Jansenism, there was a mood of sadness,
grimness, and terror. Man began to fear God. Only rarely
would he be brave enough to receive the Eucharist.

The Cistercian abbey in Port Royal became the center of Jansenism. *The Rosary to the Most Blessed Sacrament* written by one of the nuns there, which emphasized everything that separates God from man, was a testimony to the prevailing mood. God was not presented as a merciful and loving Father, but as an absolute, inaccessible, strict, and ruthless Lord. According to the Jansenistic view, because a Christian is a repentant sinner, he cannot allow himself to experience joy. His life should be dominated by the sadness that comes from remembering his own sins. Blaise Pascal's sister, the director of the girls' boarding house in Port Royal, forbade laughter in the rules for her pupils; even smiles were discouraged.

Jansenism was condemned several times by the Apostolic See, but its effects were still experienced by St. Thérèse of Lisieux who had to obtain special permission from her superior to receive Holy Communion more often. Another effect of Jansenism that appears often in a modern Christian's life is the fear of God, seeing Him only as the fair Judge. But Christian faith most fully expresses itself in the joy of discovering the personal love of God, which you can depend on and to which you can entrust yourself. Faith experienced in this way eradicates the attitude of dramatic fatalism toward one's own evil, which our contrition can change into a "happy fault." Christian joy flowing from faith is like a stream of God's love. It is faith that tells you to smile at God, to be joyful in His love. Then you should look at yourself, whom you take much too seriously, from a certain distance and with a humorous perspective. The virtue of humor lets you defeat the poison of sadness with which Satan tries to permeate your soul. This virtue of humor causes you to stop worrying about yourself and allows you to live a life of joy flowing from faith.

HUMOR AS AN "EXORCISM"

The virtue of humor, which is seeing the absurd in the world, is a religious remedy that can have the **value of an exorcism**. When you are resisting a wave of temptations, a wave of persistent thoughts that may tire you, do not fight with Satan, for he is stronger than you; instead try to deride him and scoff at him. Use this "exorcism," which is a religious sense of humor, by making fun of Satan. You can then repel his attack in the most effective way. **A ridiculed Satan is most forcefully struck** because he is deadly serious and terrified of ridicule, so he is therefore compelled to leave you.

The Christian sense of humor will also help you to fight another enemy: your own self. This is also an idol that is deadly serious, untouchable, and absolute. It cannot be meddled with or ridiculed; it cannot be offended or criticized. Using humor to fight this idol becomes a religious remedy and an act of faith when you look at yourself and try to see this self in the appropriate light: *In reality, I am truly such a small "nothing." Why, then, do I make myself the center of the universe? Why do I believe that my concerns are the most important? Why do I suffer for my defeats and troubles so much, and why am I so deadly serious?* It would suffice to look at everything with a little bit of friendly scoff: to see that what I am so worried about, what I fear, and what I care about is really silly compared to the one important reality – God.

Christian humor is a remedy that dethrones the idol of self. When you see the humor in a situation where your own self is ascending to the throne, then this situation is ridiculed and rendered harmless to you, at least for a while. Your vanity and pride become unmasked; whatever pretended to be great or was the threat arousing fear in you is ridiculed and unmasked. In this way, the religious remedy of humor also has the significant role of preserving your psychological balance.

DUST AND ASHES

Humor is a religious remedy by which you can tell yourself: *Look how absurd I am. I worry about trifles. I have so many troubles. I am ruining my health. But, in reality, everything is like ashes, like rubbish, and in the end may prove to be worthless.* Try to look at your life in the light of faith; **try to joke about yourself.** This may be difficult because the virtue of humor sometimes requires heroism. Nevertheless, it enables you to attain the proper perspective between the two realities: God and yourself. In this way, the virtue of humor cleanses your faith of egoism and strengthens it. It will show you with great clarity that only God is really important in your life. That is why you should not make yourself the center of the universe. **Perceive yourself as** a small grain of sand, as St. Thérèse spoke of herself – **a small "nothing,"** which should not be cared for, or troubled with, or worried about too much. "Pray," wrote the saint, "that the *grain of sand* become an ATOM seen only by the eyes of Jesus!"[28]

---

[28] Thérèse to Sister Agnes of Jesus, LT 74, 6 January 1889 in *Letters of Thérèse*, 1:500 (italics added by author).

The Christian sense of humor will free you from yourself. It will allow you to re-evaluate every value in the light of faith and to acknowledge that everything that happens around you is really absurdly trivial – everything except God. It will allow you to unmask those things that only seem to be values. Compared with God's value, everything is **dust and ashes** in the end – your work, your plans and your troubles, politics, and whatever happens all around you. It is in this spirit that Lent begins with the liturgy of Ash Wednesday, when the priest places ashes on your head and says that from dust you have arisen and into dust you shall return. Dust is something absurdly trivial. Not only are you dust, but so is all that you really care for and all that you are attached to, as well as all that you fear. Thanks to the virtue of humor, you will open yourself more fully to God. There will be more room for Him because you are able to see everything else in its proper perspective – as dust and ashes. It means that you are able to put all of this on the axis of absurdity.

As an example of this perspective, we can look at the conversion of St. Francis of Assisi. When he threw everything at the feet of his father in order to follow the voice of God, suddenly he was free. It was as if the whole world turned upside down: "He who has seen the whole world hanging on a hair of the Mercy of God, has seen the truth . . . He who has seen the vision of his city upside down, has seen it the right way up. The man that has seen the hierarchy turned upside down will always have something of a smile for superiorities."[29] Assisi was the birthplace and

---

[29] G. K. Chesterton, *Saint Francis of Assisi* (New York: Doubleday, Doran, 1945), 114, 115.

home of St. Francis. It was a feudal town surrounded by a moat, walls, and towers. Society in Assisi at that time was a noble pyramid made up of several social groups each subordinate to the other. There were the serious city elders, the serious noblemen, the burghers, and the serfs. And suddenly, in the eyes of Francis, this world was turned upside down and became something ridiculously insignificant. It would take only one push for Assisi's world of important city elders, lords, and noblemen to crack and collapse. All of this seen by Francis on the axis of the absurd became like dust and ashes. Before the face of God, human strength seemed ridiculous and unimportant. Francis understood that there is only one important, serious reality worth living for: God and His will. It is God's will that one must never laugh at; it should be loved. One should, as a child, trustfully hold onto what alone is important.

At the basis of most sins lies one's steadfast importance and absolute gravity. **You sin because you are so very important.** Walter Kasper wrote that casting aside this importance through Christian humor makes us capable of "an inwardly relaxed, cheerful and truly human life."[30] Humor points out the absurdity of our pretending to be important. The lack of humor and its accompanying irritability is one of the most important accusations leveled at modern Christians.

The Pharisees were people who were deadly serious; they were so very certain of their righteousness and importance. At the same time, they were so attached to their

---

[30] Kasper, *Introduction to Christian Faith*, 131.

vision of the world and of God that they reacted aggressively to accusations. Pharisaism is the opposite of simplicity. Simplicity includes freedom that flows from living in the truth and from seeing oneself in truth. At the same time, Pharisaism is a contradiction to the attitude of an evangelical child who, acknowledging his own weakness, is free of the feeling of importance. It should be remembered that a sin against the Holy Spirit, among other things, is when a person does not want to accept the truth about himself and does not acknowledge his own weakness.

Supernatural humor allows us to see the human and divine realities in the proper proportion. It allows us to gain greater distance, greater detachment, and greater freedom. **Being distanced** from occurrences and from ourselves, achieved **thanks to a sense of humor, enables us to live the Gospel more fully.** It allows us to change our priorities so that our own lives and affairs stop being so important. It allows us to avoid being extremely absorbed – to avoid excessive problems and inundation of work – in order to hear Christ's call that there is need of only one thing (cf. Lk 10:42). Owing to the virtue of humor, failures and losses do not become life's tragedies. Faith supported by humor can carry you even to the summits of detachment. Evangelical freedom is exemplified by St. Paul's principle of using the world in such a way so as not to use it, "From now on, let those having wives act as not having them, those weeping as not weeping, those rejoicing as not rejoicing, those buying as not owning, those using the world as not using it fully"

(1 Cor 7:29-31). St. John of the Cross encourages, "Endeavor always that things be not for you, nor you for them."[31]

St. Thérèse of the Child Jesus spoke of herself as a grain of sand, a small "nothing." This is how her childlike attitude was expressed; it contains none of the grave seriousness that lies at the base of many of our sins. Most of our sins toward those who are close to us are due to the fact that we become insulted and hurt over nothing. We are often oversensitive and touchy about things that concern us. All of those temperamental, oversensitive, and touchy people need a sense of humor that liberates and brings freedom from their own selves. For people overly sensitive about themselves, even the smallest detail grows to huge proportions. If we knew how to react with a sense of humor to various conflicts, arguments, and misunderstandings, and if we allowed ourselves to be laughed at a little, then how much would our humility, faith, and love grow within us. **In the light of faith, there is, however, only one important reality that must never be laughed at – God.**

Try to take yourself and what surrounds you a little less seriously, and look at all of it more in the light of faith. You will then see how often what touches you deeply is fit to be laughed at or joked about. **Try to laugh to yourself and at yourself.** Try to imitate God who must surely have a unique sense of humor. Just consider that He has chosen you as His partner in the great work that He does. Is this not an expression of His unique sense of humor?

---

[31] *The Sayings of Light and Love*, in *The Collected Works of St. John of the Cross*, 92.

A SAINT WITH HUMOR

The virtue of humor in the saints reached such a degree of heroism that it radiated even in the face of great suffering or death. Sir Thomas More, a saintly man, but still only a man, experienced psychophysical fears that arose in him just as we experience them. No one is free from fears; even our Savior experienced them. Sir Thomas most certainly feared the quartering and torture that he was told he would suffer. Later, the sentence of torture was changed to beheading. On the day of the execution, Sir Thomas More changed into his best clothes, and the lieutenant, seeing this, demanded that he dress down. Finally, Sir Thomas had to comply. He was then brought out of the Tower of London and led to the place of execution. Before he walked onto the scaffold, the mood was very somber and difficult to endure. A religious remedy of humor was needed. Thomas More then said to the officer in charge of the execution, who was also deadly serious, "I pray you, Mr. Lieutenant, see me safely up, and for my coming down let me shift for myself."[32] This quip expresses his humor even in the face of his own death.

King Henry VIII had forbidden him to speak – it is obvious how a person such as this could affect the people, a person whose sense of humor did not abandon him even in the face of death. What power this is! Even Satan fears a person with a true sense of religious humor, let alone Henry VIII. There was, therefore, no speech. The prisoner knelt and after saying a prayer, turned to his executioner and, with a

---

[32] "Roper's Life of More," in *The Utopia of Sir Thomas More* (Roslyn, New York: Walter J. Black, 1947), 279.

cheerful expression, said to him, "Pluck up thy spirits, man, and be not afraid to do thine office. My neck is very short. Take heed, therefore, thou strike not awry for saving thine honor."[33] Those were the last words of Thomas More; he was able to laugh at himself – to put himself, his concerns, and even his own death, on the axis of the absurd. Since before God – the one reality for whom it is worth living – even our own death is unimportant. Sir Thomas More must have truly had the soul of a child holding his Father's hand very tightly to be able to joke in the face of his own death. This was done by one who had often prayed for a Christian sense of humor.

---

[33] Ibid., 280.

CHAPTER SEVEN

TRIALS OF FAITH

In order for faith to become strong, it must be tried. It must go through a crucible of experiences, through many trials and storms. A shallow faith dependent solely on education, feelings, and certain habits, collapses in the face of difficulties. In trials of faith, God wants a person who believes to become stripped of what is not faith but is only a support of faith. God wants a person to be stripped of what is not true adherence to Christ, what is not reliance on Him, and what is not the entrustment of oneself to Him.

True faith is free from all natural supports such as understanding, feelings, and intellectual or imaginative experiences. True faith is dependent solely on Him and on His word. God does not accept a situation by which you base your faith on your actions, your feelings, or your experiences. Therefore He allows trials of faith that differ depending on what, besides God, you place your faith. If you rely on your natural understanding, all clearness of your reason must vanish. At a certain point, what you have believed in starts to make no sense. If you have placed your faith in certain people – laymen or clergymen, and their actions – then even this, at a certain point, must sway or collapse. If your faith has relied on feelings – on the satisfaction and joy experienced in prayer or religious practices – then you must not be surprised when a time comes of spiritual dryness and an aversion to those practices. You have to go through this painful cleansing in order to gain a pure, true faith and, eventually, true contemplation.

HUNGER FOR GOD

God, by placing man in difficult situations, provokes him into performing acts of faith. These situations, which make us realize our powerlessness, can deepen our yearning for God. God does not want to come to us uninvited. **Love wants to be looked for**; otherwise, love is pushed away. In this sense, **faith looks for God to come.** The intensity of looking for God to come indicates the greatness of faith in His power and His love. You can never look enough for God to come. Faith intensifies due to your attempts to look for Him to come. However, this occurs primarily due to God's grace that causes your yearning for Him to grow and deepen within you. God has His ways to enliven your looking for Him and for His graces that follow.

There are two specific categories of these ways of God. First, He can stir the desire within your heart for His coming, for example, through some creative anxiety or great need. Faith will then be expressed by a need for God. Growth of faith will be indicated by your **increasingly intense looking for God to come and your hungering for Him**. At other times, He may allow or cause you to go through difficult **trials of faith** when you will not be able to cope with your problems by yourself. These could, for example, be moral problems, sins that you commit, family problems such as a crumbling marriage, or a problem with a son who gets drunk, who is living with someone outside of marriage, or who is an unbeliever. These trials could be problems with health that could suddenly fail you or someone close to you. The experience of not being able to cope with something, and the feeling of loss, can cause you to have the desire to look for His coming. This is a chance for the growth and the deepening of your faith. All of these difficulties and problems that God allows or causes to come into your life are meant to awaken the hunger for God in you; they are trials of faith. Looking at all of this in the light of faith, you will come to know the "spirituality of events" that says that every event is God passing by. Certain experiences of God passing by are oriented toward awakening in you the desire for His presence, His help, and His redemptive intervention. The more you feel ill, the more you feel the need for a doctor. The more you feel helpless and crushed by various difficulties, the greater the desire within you for the coming of Him who can help you, who imparts His redemptive grace to all of your problems, and who can save you. All you need to do is believe that He wants to give you everything you need, to believe in His might and boundless love.

When God wants you to reach the depths of faith, He can give you very difficult trials; He can take much away from you and even strip you of many supports. God may want you to become uprooted so that, not having any human securities, you can look for redemptive help to come from Him alone.

THE FAITH OF ABRAHAM

Abraham, the father of our faith, is the patron of our looking for God to come. How did God make Abraham look for Him to come? God uprooted him. According to the Bible, God's first call was, "Go forth from the land of your kinsfolk and from your father's house to a land that I will show you" (Gen 12:1). So Abraham, rooted in his native Haran not far from Ur in the Chaldeans, obeyed God. And when he departed from his native land and became stripped of every support, he had no choice but to listen intently to the Word of God. In this way his faith grew because Abraham became increasingly more reliant on the will of God, and asked **what God expected from him**. And, in this way, a new phenomenon appeared in the history of mankind – a phenomenon of Christian faith resulting from the call of God to a person and from the existential nakedness of man. Abraham's faith and self-entrustment to God were born from being uprooted and from the uncertainty experienced by him. Abraham, a man of faith, was born and grew to maturity. Our birth into faith will not be easy either. It will also be a result of trials and difficulties – a result of our nakedness, of threatening situations, and of there being nothing to rely on.

God is a God of promises and blessings. Abraham received the promise of a land, descendants, and a special blessing from God. However, it was not a clear promise, but one clouded with a certain darkness. God said, "Go forth…to a land that I will show you," (Gen 12:1) but Abraham had never seen this land because a free land, or one that was waiting for his arrival, did not exist. Abraham did not know how this promise from God would be fulfilled, but he **entrusted this to his Lord**. Such was the greatness of faith in Abraham. The promise of descendants was also unclear since he was an old man. From a human point of view, this seemed rather unlikely. Abraham had to believe in something that in human terms seemed impossible.

The more God's promise seems unlikely, the more God demands and expects from us, but the greater will be the merit of our trusting response. The promise made to Abraham was so improbable that he had to believe that God is a God of impossible and improbable things. For Abraham, achieving this belief would be a long, continual process of growing in faith. When he reached the Promised Land, it was not his to keep. He would always be a stranger. However, the greatest deepening of his faith came under more dramatic conditions. God demanded of him the sacrifice of his son, which was the sacrifice of someone who was most dear to him. From a human point of view, his son was his greatest treasure and was of the greatest value to him. This situation was incredibly difficult. Therefore, Abraham must have expected that God would somehow resolve this terrifying situation caused by His demand. Abraham had to decide to trust boundlessly. The demand God made of Abraham struck at his fatherly feelings, at his great love for his only beloved son. At the same time, God struck Abraham at the very foundation of the faith he had held until then. Abraham had believed that many descendants would come from his son. What God demanded of him must have seemed all the more absurd. The one from whom so many promised descendants were to be born was now to be killed. God demanded so much from Abraham because He wanted to grant him something special: **He wanted to raise his trust to the peak.** Abraham's trial of faith was not really a test; God already knew how Abraham would react. This trial provoked him to make a decision so that, in darkness, he would trust God in a special way. In this way, **he moved forward toward Him on his pilgrimage of faith.** The most difficult situations are of a particular advantage since they demand crucial decisions. **Faith develops through decisions** by which man devotes himself to God through the "obedience of faith."[34]

You will also undergo a trial like that of Abraham because, in loving you, God will at some time place you in a difficult situation. He will allow or cause something to be a great burden for you and extremely difficult for you to bear. You will be unable to cope with it. This is so that you will begin to look for Him to come, and so that you will desire Him. He will make it impossible for you to remain in a state of religious stagnation. The trial of faith that you will encounter will then force your faith to be polarized. You will either not respond to God's desire and begin to retreat in your faith or, like Abraham, you will decide to entrust yourself to Him in the darkness of faith. Then your faith, your hunger for Christ and His Redemption, and your hunger for grace

---

[34] Second Vatican Council, *Dei Verbum* (Dogmatic Constitution on Divine Revelation), no. 5 [Proclaimed by Pope Paul VI on November 18, 1965].

will grow in you. To the extent of this hunger, the Holy Spirit will be able to descend into your heart.

TRIALS OF FAITH IN THE LIFE OF MARY

The Church begins the calendar year with a day dedicated to the Blessed Mother. On the first of January we are shown the figure of her who "advanced in her pilgrimage of faith."[35] In Mary's life, the blessing said to her by Elizabeth, "Blessed are you who believed" (Lk 1:45), was brought about every day. Therefore the Church sees Mary as the most complete example for our faith.

Mary goes before us, leading the way on the "pilgrimage of faith," as if she were anticipating our steps. Mary is near us on our road to faith. According to conciliar thought, the Blessed Mother is pre-eminent and wholly unique in the Church,[36] while, at the same time, she is closest to us. It could be said that we hurt the Blessed Mother when we speak only of her eminence and elevation and, by so doing, create a distance between her and us. Too much is said about her distinctiveness and too little about the fact that **she is our way and this way is Christocentric**. Mary is our way in the sense that she goes before us and shows us the way of faith, for she has already experienced everything that could happen to us. Looking at her life, we should find answers to our problems.

---

[35] Second Vatican Council, *Lumen Gentium* (Dogmatic Constitution of the Church), no. 58 [Proclaimed by Pope Paul VI on November 21, 1964] (hereafter cited as LG).
[36] LG, no. 53.

When we speak only about the nobleness and exaltation of the Blessed Mother, we treat her the way hagiographers often treated the saints. Someone once said that the saints suffered most, not at the hands of their persecutors, but at the hands of hagiographers who, by removing their simple human characteristic from their biographies, made them up to be sugary, lifeless figures. It is not enough to honor Mary, to venerate her, and to place a crown on her head. These are "rich means," which she never used in her life. To love Mary means to imitate her and follow her because she is the one who goes before us, the one who is an example for our faith.

If we are surprised that God foils our plans and leads us down a different road than the one we imagined, let us recall that it was the same in the life of the Blessed Mother. Mary also thought of her sanctity, her road, her mission differently. The one who gave up motherhood was called to an exceptional and unique motherhood. This call foiled all of her plans. By responding to the Annunciation with her *yes*, Mary did not fully realize what she was agreeing to. However, that did not diminish the value of her consent, which she later confirmed with her continual *yes* throughout her life. God so loved Mary that He chose this very harsh way of treating her. We know that this is the way He treats His friends. This is the best method for allowing the shaping of a person in the image of the Son of God.

Let us look at the way God formed Mary's faith through the "hurricanes" during her life and by the difficulty of her trials. Shortly after Mary's first *fiat*, when it was announced to her that she would conceive and bear the Son of God, it turned out that St. Joseph knew nothing about it. This was the first tragedy for both of these people. Mary and Joseph did not know what to do, and they suffered greatly because of this. It must have been a shock to Joseph when he realized that Mary was with child, and it was also a torment for her. Surely it would not have been difficult for God to explain the situation to Joseph. During this time, Mary must have been continually asking herself, *What shall I do?* This was a difficult time full of darkness for her.

Faith does not remove darkness; it does just the opposite: it requires it. This truth reveals the meaning of faith. The Blessed Mother, living in faith, lived in great darkness and was therefore tested in her faith in a sometimes exceptionally hard manner. The birth of Jesus in Bethlehem was a trial of this kind. The time and place of childbirth is a sensitive issue for every mother. A mother wants to give birth in a worthy place, under humane conditions – this is her basic right. Did Mary not long for this? However, it was not granted to her. If Jesus had to be born in Bethlehem, would it not have been easier for Mary if Joseph had learned about this in advance? He was being given instructions in his sleep anyway, so he could have also received the instruction: *Go to Bethlehem for that is where the Child will be born.* Instead, God decided to arrange things in a different way. The Child Jesus was born in Bethlehem due to the unusual circumstance of a census. Consequently, in this situation, Jesus was born under very poor conditions, without any securities. Because of the crowds of newcomers, it was hard to find any room. It would have been so easy then to succumb to the temptation of doubt and fear. And it was in the difficult situation of this trial of faith that the child was to be born. The angel appeared to Mary only during the Annunciation. After that there were no further instructions, no further messages or mission. During the birth of Jesus, the angels appeared only to the shepherds tending their flocks, not to Mary. Soon after, along with the coming of the Three Wise Men, the next "earthquake" came — the persecution by Herod. This was a difficult trial of faith when questions such as these may arise: *Why is God silent? Why does He not intervene to defend His Son? Why does He appear powerless in the face of Herod's tyranny? And why is it necessary to escape to an unknown land where there is no human support?*

The next trial of faith that proved to be very difficult arose when the young Jesus remained in the temple without previously telling His parents. The Gospel says that they did not understand the words He spoke to them when they found Him; Mary only kept them in her heart. Thus darkness continued in her life. Why did Jesus not want to explain anything to her? She, **the Mother of God, had to learn the correct way to interpret events**. She had to learn the spirituality of events. God did not make anything easier for her; everything in her life was always very difficult.

The *yes* during the Annunciation seems joyous and easy compared to the last *yes* spoken under the Cross. A person on a high level in his spiritual life is usually ready to sacrifice his own self. It is much more difficult to agree to the suffering of those close to us, the ones we love very much. Mary, standing at the Cross, gave a double *yes*: **let it so happen to us, to Him and to me.** *If my beloved Son is to suffer and be tortured, then let it be so.* Agreeing to this was the supreme sacrifice. This *fiat* of Mary at the Cross caused her to become the Mother of the Church and the Mother of us all. **That most difficult *yes* was the source of Mary's spiritual motherhood.** If you are very upset or depressed by something, remember that you are then close to Mary whose life was so very difficult. God loved Mary in a special, exceptional way, but in her life there was so much suffering. God treats His friends in just this way.

It is a special form of God's love and trust toward us whenever God wants us not to expect Him to show us His feelings, so that He is free to act. We can imagine an ideal marriage in which a husband is very busy with some kind of work. The wife who loves him does not want to bother him with anything. On her own she finds the materials he needs, trying to help him the best she can. She thinks only of him. This "gift of self for love" is shown when a person, thinking about someone else, diminishes himself by not seeking any attention for himself. This is an unusually difficult love. This is the kind of love Christ demanded of His mother.

This kind of love is portrayed in the evangelical scene of the encounter of Jesus with His mother and closest family. He was told, "Your mother and your brothers are standing outside, asking to speak with you" (Mt 12:47). Jesus treated His mother then in a way He could treat only the person He loved very much, the one He had the utmost trust in. He spoke as if He were refusing her, "Who is my mother? Who are my brothers?" (Mt 12:48). It may have seemed that Christ was very brusque toward His mother. But all of these were her trials, trials of her total devotion to God. For Mary, this harsh treatment was the expression of the highest trust shown toward her by her Son. Mary knew that Jesus was counting on her, and she did not expect to be particularly honored by Him. Mary never stood in the way of Jesus' apostolic mission, and this was evidence of her great, selfless love for her Son. If He sometimes seems harsh to you, it means that He loves you very much and trusts that you will not disappoint Him and leave. Christ continually stripped His mother of her supports, and she continued to say *yes* to Him. She became increasingly like the divine example of her Son.

Can this life be described as a very difficult one? Yes and no. This ambivalence occurs because these **events of being stripped of supports can become joy and happiness** for a person who loves God and is united with Him. That is **because they are an opportunity to profess one's love for God and prove one's loyalty and faith in Him.**

Whenever it is difficult for you and He remains silent, remember that this silence is just another form of His word, and His absence is just another form of His permanent overwhelming Presence. When it seems to us that Jesus is silent and absent, it is not really so. This is indicated by the words God told St. Teresa of Avila, "When you thought that you were alone, I was nearest to you." When you feel very alone, when it is hard for you, when you are experiencing some kind of nakedness, He is closest to you. However, He does not give you signs because He wants you to trust in Him even more. **This kind of silence and seeming absence is a risk for Him.** Some people then leave. At one time, a great number of people who were listening to Jesus left because they thought that Jesus was demanding too much of them. Leaving Jesus because of trials of faith happens again and again. Some come through trials strengthened by trusting in God; others walk away from Him.

Mary's attitude in the face of such difficult trials of faith awakens our guilty conscience. In her life, all trials of faith ended with a deepening of her self-entrustment to God. Although she went through so many difficult experiences, she never failed God. In Mary there was no discrepancy between the ideal and its realization. God's ideal was brought about in her life so fully that she became God's masterpiece, the most perfect realization of His plans. We, on the other hand, constantly create a dissonance between our faith and life, between our words and deeds, between our ideals and their realization. As the result of trials of faith, we retreat or we may even leave. It is in this sense that the example of Mary awakens our guilty conscience.

Mary, who serves as an example of trusting abandonment to God, could be called the Blessed Mother of Acceptance, or the Mother of Abandonment to God, since she continually said to God, *Let it happen the way You want.* The most important event in the history of the world happened in the darkness of the night in Gethsemane. This event was Christ's *yes* spoken to His Father. The most important events in your life will occur when, just as Mary did, you choose the way of continually giving consent to God. Her consent extended throughout her entire life. It should also be the same for you. Your life is comprised of continual annunciations, understood as calls of grace and as trials of faith. Time is priceless because it is the presence of God. The current moment is a call directed to us. It is a trial of faith. It is God's question, *Will you say yes to me?* Our life in faith is brought down to this *yes*. **The essence of Christianity is the continual saying to God, *Thy will be done*.** The Blessed Mother continually repeated these words to God. Can anyone love more than she did?

Mary was always full of grace and, at the same time, she continually grew in grace. Through loyalty and trust, this special human soul became like a vessel that, despite always being full of grace, was able to continually receive more. Is this not a paradox? It was as if God continually expanded her heart, and every new trial of faith, every *yes*, caused her to grow in grace. The Blessed Mother's life, ordinary and gray, was being sanctified with this continuous *fiat*.

The distance between Mary and us is always brought about through our fault. It is we who make her unreachable and distant. It is this very distance that accuses us of mediocrity, minimalism, compromise, and fear of responding to grace completely. It is much easier to say that she was immaculately conceived, that she was the Mother of God, that she was exceptional, and that I cannot imitate her. But these are only excuses and the setting up of obstacles to the impelling call of grace to follow in her footsteps.

We could ask why it is so important to Jesus that we follow in Mary's footsteps, to go toward Him in her way. One of the answers to this question is the radicalism of the Blessed Mother, the radicalism of a devotion to God that makes possible God's offering of Himself to us. Jesus loved Mary in an unusual and exceptional way. He loved no other creature as He loved her because she was able to give everything to Him. She, who had chosen virginity, accomplished this, not only in the sense of maintaining chastity in celibacy, but also in complete devotion to God out of love. Mary's evangelical virginity consists in her determined will to live in chastity in order to completely devote herself to God and live for Him. From the first moment of her existence, Mary adhered to the Everlasting Word with all the strength of her will and love. And it is in this way that Mary realized the highest ideal of virginity in her life. Mary, through abandoning herself to God without reservation and in a perfect way, became first the Bride and then the Mother of the Word.

God offers Himself to the soul to the extent with which it devotes itself to Him. Then how complete must have been the Word's offering of Himself to Mary if she so totally became a gift for Him. **Mary's is the type of soul that Jesus particularly loved for its total abondonment to Him.** Jesus wants us to choose Mary's way because He wants us to fulfill our lives by having the type of soul He loves for its total devotion. His deep desire is to find souls similar to hers – souls who follow Him to the end – and to overwhelm them with the infinite wellspring of His love and His graces. The desire to find souls such as this is His "hunger," which is never satisfied within Him. He calls you to go Mary's way in order to reveal the greatness of His desires for you.

If you imitate Mary and become increasingly like her, then Jesus will be able, to the extent of your devotion, to love you with the same love with which He loved her. Mary stands before you as the type of soul fully devoted to God. Mary's example calls you to bring about the ideal of a radicalism of faith.

STORMS IN OUR LIVES

An especially privileged time for the development of our faith is when we experience storms in our lives. The storm at sea described in the Gospel is a certain symbol for our situation. During difficult trials of faith, in the times of lesser or greater storms, it seems to us that Jesus has abandoned us, that He is not there. There can be various storms: the storms of temptations, storms of scruples, storms of worrying about the future, about health, about work, and storms involving discord in marriage. In the face of a storm, two types of attitudes can be observed: fear, as in the case of the terrified apostles, and peace, symbolized by Jesus sleeping in the boat. Jesus was sleeping through a human tragedy in a boat tossed by the waves and in danger of sinking at any moment. He must have been tired, but was it only His fatigue? Jesus slept in the apostles' boat and they thought that everything was lost. This is where their panic, stress, and terror had come from when they woke Jesus. During that storm two attitudes were revealed: the faces of the apostles contorted in fear and the peaceful face of Jesus who was sleeping. Christ's attitude seemed so strange that the apostles accused Him, "Teacher, do you not care that we are perishing?" (Mk 4:38).

Every storm has its purpose. It is God passing by, which will bring with it some great grace – primarily the grace of trust. During a storm you should direct the eyes of your faith on the peaceful face of Christ. A "theology" of God's sleep can be discussed here. **During our storms God seems to be sleeping**. The revelation of the Bible includes not only God's word but also God's gestures. How very rich in context is this gesture of Jesus sleeping during the dramatic moment of threat. Of course, this does not mean that when threatened with danger one should do nothing. Quietism is contradictory to the teaching of the Church. Jesus does not reproach the apostles because they tried to save the boat. He accused them of the lack of an attitude of faith, which caused them to succumb to the temptation of fear or even panic. It is with this gesture of sleep that He wanted to tell them, *But I am with you, you should be calm, for nothing can happen to a boat that I am in.*

The attitude of faith is simultaneously a prayer of faith. It is expressed by calmness in the face of danger, by peace on a spiritual level since we have no direct influence on our psychophysical level. There will be many anxieties that will tear us apart, but that is not important. What is important is that fear, aroused at an emotional and mental level, does not control our spiritual level. It is important that it does not cause a change in our attitude, deeds, thoughts, and desires. Our faith and our belief in the fact that He is present here, close to us, makes us calm in spite of our emotional state. His presence is a presence of eternal power and eternal love. When storms come into your life, internal or external, look at the peaceful face of Jesus. Then you will understand that you are not alone and that, in every situation, He is saying, *This storm will pass; it has to pass.*

During our storms and our trials of faith, we must also never forget about the continuous presence of Mary who is close to us as the Mother of our abandonment to God. Let us ask her to allow us to share in her abandonment to God, so that we may stop trusting ourselves, things, and people, and that we may perceive the continuous presence of her Son who is close to us and is our only security. We ask Mary that, following her example, we trust exclusively in the Lord: *Mother of Great Abandonment, I offer myself to you without reservation – to the end.*

ANXIETY ARISING FROM A LACK OF FAITH

Trials of faith do not always strengthen faith or make it more dynamic. If you reject the stripping of yourself that is connected with the trials, then you retreat from entrusting yourself to God. Your faith, in the face of difficulties, will start to collapse. Your life will be dominated by anxiety, haste, and stress – symptoms of an immature faith or the lack of it, which negate the very life of faith.

When you succumb to haste, anxiety, and stress in the face of trials of faith, which may be some kind of threat or difficulty, you wound the love of Jesus. When you take these difficult matters into your own hands and want to solve them on your own, **you simply count on yourself**, and then there is no room for faith. Faith is the reliance on His might and His boundless love. When you allow anxiety, haste, or stress to overcome you, it is as though you were pushing Jesus aside and as if you were saying, *I cannot count on You now; I have to take this matter into my own hands.*

Of course, you have to differentiate between the two levels in a person: the psychophysical level and the spiritual level. The psychophysical level of a person, the level of a person's feelings, is the first to be overcome by haste, anxiety, and stress in the face of difficulties and threats. As long as the inner tension that pushes you to haste or anxiety remains at the psychophysical level you do not hurt Jesus. However, you may allow your mentally difficult situation, and all the anxiety or haste coming from it, to overcome your spiritual faculties, which are your thoughts and your will. This already reveals your unfaithfulness and lack of faith. It does not mean that you should remove fear, haste or anxiety from your psychophysical level, for often this is impossible. It does mean that there should be no panic in your attitude, which is determined and formed by your spiritual sphere, so that peace flowing from faith can dominate there.

It is not easy to maintain an attitude of peace. Saints also had to struggle often with difficulties of this kind. For example, St. Maximillian had stomach ulcers, which may suggest that he might have experienced nervous tension. There was a time in his life when he actually ordered himself to be calm in the face of threats. Thus he had to fight for his faith.

The virtue of fortitude does not necessarily consist in our not feeling fear or anxiety on the psychophysical level. It does consist in our not succumbing to that fear. It means believing that we are never alone, that there is always Someone with us who loves us and upon whom everything is dependent. Difficult graces of trials of faith, often involving suffering, should be accepted by us with the awareness of the closeness of Christ. We should accept them with the belief that He will be victorious, that after Good Friday, Resurrection Sunday will come. There should be an unshaken faith within us that He who is peace, power, joy, and the Resurrection is with us even more during our trials and suffering.

Living by the present moment, sanctifying it as a moment of grace, is an expression of the dynamism of our faith and of our fight with the temptations of anxiety, haste, and stress. "Surrender yourself totally into the hands of the Merciful Providence, that is, into the hands of the Immaculate, and be at peace," wrote St. Maximillian to one of the brothers in the convent.[37] Live as if this were your last day. Tomorrow is uncertain, yesterday does not belong to you – only today is yours. God does not want you to look back because then you more often succumb to those temptations of fear, haste, and stress. "No one who sets a hand to the plow and looks to what was left behind is fit for the kingdom of God" (Lk 9:62). Nor does God want you to worry about the future. In the Sermon on the Mount, Jesus clearly states, "Sufficient for a day is its own evil" (Mt 6:34). If you look back at the past or look to the future, you are not living the present moment; you lose the "grace of the moment" that He wants to bestow upon you.

To live in the present moment can be visualized through a certain fictional scene that is like a parable. Imagine that you are standing on a platform and a long train is passing by with many empty cars that you have to load with the packages lying beside you. When you start looking at the cars that have passed, you may notice with fright the multitude of cars that have not been loaded – you are thinking about the past. Then you look at the ones that are approaching you, and again become frightened that there are still so many cars left to be loaded – you are thinking about the future. **In the meantime, however, another car has**

---

[37] K. Strzelecka, *Maksymilian Maria Kolbe*.

passed by unloaded – you are letting the present moment, and the graces connected with it, slip by.

Anxieties that nag you about the past or the future are also trials of faith. God expects that you will offer Him all of these anxieties so that you can entrust yourself more fully to Him and totally abandon yourself to Him.

PEACE BORN OF FAITH

If trials of faith strengthen your self entrustment to Jesus – your adherence to Him and your reliance on Him – His peace will enter your life. The words **"peace be with you"** (Hebrew: *shalom*) is a very intimate greeting that wishes you peace stemming from an intimate communion with God. This is how it was understood in the Old Testament. Christ greeted His disciples with this very greeting: *shalom*. During the Last Supper, He said to them, "Peace I leave with you; my peace I give to you. Not as the world gives do I give it to you" (Jn 14:27).

The world also wants to give us peace, but only human peace. There are two kinds of peace, just like there are two kinds of happiness. There is human peace and human happiness, both of which are short-lived and temporary. On the other hand, there is Christ's peace and Christ's happiness, which are born in us as a permanent reality when based on faith. What is this human peace and human happiness? It is something we obtain from people. We obtain it as though it were given to us out of pity from another person. In other words, looking for this kind of peace and happiness is like begging for scraps. These small bits of human esteem, a hint of praise, a compliment or someone's positive perception of us, are simply scraps on which we want to build our peace. Sometimes a person manages to get what he wants; he gains others' esteem or becomes successful, and gains this common human scrap that gives him some satisfaction. This is the human peace, begged for, which the world gives. But how fleeting this peace is! It does not take much for our human peace to dissipate and for our happiness to vanish. It is enough that someone is rude to us, is vindictive, or gives us a suspicious glance. There is no longer peace within us because the scraps we begged for are taken from us.

When there is no human peace left, fear – its opposite – appears. Fear promotes sickness and causes neurosis. Fear is born out of the seeking of human peace. It is a result of losing those bits of peace for which we begged and which were taken from us. At other times, fear is the consequence of losing someone's esteem or positive perception of us, or not receiving a sincere smile and a small acceptance of our deeds. In this way, we have become dependent on human whims and moods, on what "makes our day" and on that which the world gives us.

The second peace, **the peace of Christ, flows from His presence**. It is His gift. "My peace I give to you," (Jn 14:27) says Christ. He is our peace given to us through faith (cf. Eph 2:14). **Accepting peace from Christ through faith is accepting His person; it is totally opening the door of our hearts to Him.**

Anxiety and sadness are always bad and always flow from self-love. But peace and happiness do not always come from Christ. Not every peace is good, just as not every joy is good. If you are glad that you yourself have accomplished something, then this is a human, very short-lived happiness – a piece of scrap. If we strive for this type of happiness and this kind of peace, then it will always be like a bubble that can burst for no reason because our Lord does not allow our human peace, the peace of this world, to be something lasting in our life.

True peace is the fruit of spiritual life, the fruit of faith deepened as a result of trials. We receive this peace not at the start, but at the finish. True peace is not so much the evidence of achievement, but the result of a choice. If there are idols in your life – attachments and enslavements that hamper you – there will be no peace. **When something or someone stands between you and God, you cannot fully adhere to God through faith.** Moreover, there will be no peace in you. It would be a pity for you to succumb to the suffering flowing from this.

The peace of Christ comes as a result of your choosing Him. This basic choice, which is called the fundamental option, is the most important one. Is Christ really of the greatest value to you? He redeemed you on the Cross and was raised, giving you the opportunity to gain true peace and true happiness. This kind of peace evoking permanent joy is within your grasp, thanks to the sacrifice on the Cross and the Resurrection. You, however, must make a choice. You have to choose Christ with His peace by taking advantage of the fruits of the Cross and the Resurrection. This should be a process of your acceptance of Christ. You cannot choose peace and happiness if you have not chosen Christ. However, He Himself helps you with this choice by taking away whatever hampers and enslaves you. He overthrows your idols. When you accept that, then this will be your choice – your declaration for peace, happiness, and freedom. It will be the choice made by your faith.

If you are a neurotic person and perhaps getting worse, then it may mean that there is still not enough spiritual life in you, your choice of Christ is not complete. It may mean that you are still not choosing your Heavenly Friend, and there is still not enough faith that begets peace in you. You have to learn acceptance, which is to continually choose Christ. By accepting His will, you choose and accept His love.

In the end, the most important thing, the foundation of this choice, is **believing in love**. What does Jesus expect from me, what does He want? He wants you, by loving His will, to want what is best for you. Christ does not need anything for Himself. If He does want something from you, then it is always that which is best for you. He wants to love you and wants you to accept His desire, which is His love. You are like a small child that does not know what is good for him. A small child needs to be persuaded to study, to eat, to get dressed, because a child does not know how to love himself. It is the mom and dad who love him and care for him. A child is unable to love himself and care for himself. It is the same with us. We do not know what is good for us; we are unable to truly love ourselves. We love ourselves in a pure and unselfish way when we love His will, His love, and His concern for us.

Christ is someone who expects something from you. Primarily He is the Will that reveals Itself to us. **To believe and love Christ is to love what He wants, that is, to love His will.** We are to choose Him in this very way: loving what He loves. Only loving Christ's will, confirmed by our choices during trials of faith, will bring us the peace and true happiness that no one can take away from us.

CHAPTER EIGHT

THE DESERT

I n biblical symbolism, the desert is a stage on the way
toward God. All who are called on the path of faith must
go through this stage. Abraham went through it when he left
Haran in the Chaldeans to search for the Promised Land.
The history of Moses began in the desert when God
appeared to him in the burning bush and, in the quiet of the
desert, called him to the special mission of freeing the
Chosen People. Elijah also went into the desert to flee for his
life. In order to give Elijah special instructions, God told him
to wander in the desert for forty days and forty nights until
He finally revealed Himself in the middle of the desert in a
tiny whispering sound. God revealed Himself to Elijah not in
noise, not in a windstorm or an earthquake, but in the quiet
of nature and in the stillness of his heart. He revealed

Himself, not in the moment of excitement, but in silence when, free from problems and fear, Elijah remained alone with God. When speaking through the prophet Hosea, God talks about Israel as if it were His chosen bride whom He leads into the desert with love, "So I will allure her; / I will lead her into the desert / and speak to her heart" (Hos 2:16). God in His love leads a person into the desert because the desert is His gift. The desert brings about what St. Augustine asked for when he prayed, "Lord Jesus, let me know myself and know You."

THE SYMBOLISM OF THE DESERT

A desert, as either a geographical terrain or as a symbol of someone's situation, initially may not fully reveal its distinguishing characteristics. A geographical desert begins gradually. There is an increasing amount of sand, fewer and fewer trees, and more and more dunes. At the beginning, it might be possible to find an oasis. A human desert often appears in a similar way. Only selected elements of the desert might appear in one's life, or the human desert may appear in its entirety with complete nakedness and a storm of temptations – and with the special presence of the merciful God. Every difficult situation may be a desert in the sense of being a trial of faith that calls one to live by faith. There could be, for example, difficulties arising from a relationship with another person, sickness, a depressing feeling of isolation, or any other very difficult situation. A desert, *par excellence* (in the fullest sense of its meaning), can be a difficult spiritual state full of dryness for you. Then it may seem as though God has left you – you do not feel His presence, and His presence becomes that much harder to believe in.

The desert can be "imposed" by God on a person or on a community when He Himself leads someone into it; it can also be a desert by choice. It may happen that you yourself desire the situation of a desert to seek out quietness and God's presence, and you strive to be stripped of attachments. You will then meet your Enemy there, but you will, first and foremost, encounter God. **You will be able to look inside your inner self and discover the truth about yourself and, at the same time, discover what is of the utmost importance – the truth about God.** Jesus, before entering His public life, first went into the desert as if to say to you, *Look, you are not alone; I have been here before you. I was also hungry for forty days, and it was hard for me, too. You are never alone. Try to believe in my love.*

The desert can have a social character. For example, it may be experienced by an entire nation. However, it may also be the desert for an individual person. One thing is certain: **if you enter it, you will change**. It is also certain that **at some point in time you must enter it**. There will be a time when, through internal or external experiences, God will place you in a difficult situation, maybe even an extreme one, in which you will have to choose. You must then remember that this is a grace, the grace of the desert. If you are presently in a desert such as this, you should be grateful to God. Thank Him that it is difficult for you, that you are sick or lonely or not understood, or maybe that life at home or at work is like a nightmare, or that you are unable to cope with yourself. Such situations are the elements of a desert. Try to see that God, who loves you, is present in all of this.

"I WISH YOU WERE EITHER HOT OR COLD"

The desert is a place of trial, a place where human attitudes become polarized. Once four good friends, students, planned to go to the Libyan Desert. They intended to cross it in a Jeep. The events occurred as if in a movie. They were in the desert for the first time and they soon started to lose their way. Then a dramatic incident happened: the Jeep broke down and they were at a loss about what to do next. Their only recourse was to wait to be rescued. The desert, as everybody knows, terrifies and is horrible, especially when there are no prospects for the future. During the day it was mercilessly hot; at night it was intensely cold. In addition, food was getting scarce and there was barely any water. Therefore tension continued to mount. The remaining water had to be divided among four people. There was so little of it that they all nervously watched the hands of the one who was pouring it. And then something terrible happened. The hand of the one pouring, certainly because of the pressure of being watched, trembled and a little water spilled onto the sand. The tension and the nervousness of the traveling companions transformed into uncontrolled aggression – *how dare you spill it; we will die thanks to you!* Then everything came down like an avalanche. Emotions prevailed. The rest of the water was spilled and the bodies of the fighting friends rolled in the sand. When they finally realized what they were doing, one of them could not get up; he had been suffocated. This, indeed, was terrible. After all that had happened, the arrival of a helicopter, which picked up the three living men and the corpse of the fourth, was no longer important to them. What was important was that something terrible had happened between them, that they were no longer the same people. In the Libyan Desert a murder had been committed among friends who had earlier thought that they were ready to give up their lives for one another.

The situation of a desert reveals what is deeply hidden in a person. It reveals the layers of human passions and evil that manifest themselves only in difficult situations. Hence, the desert uncovers a person and reveals the truth about him. In the desert a person sees what his powerlessness, sinfulness, and unrepentant heart is capable of. **A person stands face to face there with the terrifying truth of who he really is without the visible power of God.** The barrenness of the desert uncovers the wretchedness of a person and reveals his nakedness because his illusions dissipate and there is nowhere to hide. A person can live skin deep as if on the surface of his own self. Only difficult situations and the experience of the "desert" force a person to make decisions that reveal the deep layers of good or evil.

The desert not only reveals the truth about yourself, but it also transforms you internally and polarizes your attitudes. **The gift of the desert lets you overcome lukewarmness** because the desert forces you to make choices. By making choices, you will become aware of what you are capable and, thereby, you will come to understand the two most important realities: the reality of the incomprehensible love and infinite mercy of God, as well as the reality of your own sinfulness and helplessness. As long as you are a lukewarm

Christian for whom everything goes well and for whom there are no problems, your situation, as seen in the light of faith, is tragic. You manage your life yourself and you no longer need God. This is a situation of practical atheism, which you may not even be aware of.

The ultimate reason for leading a human being, a nation, or a community into the desert is revealed by the very clearly expressed words of Revelation, "I know your works; I know that you are neither cold nor hot. I wish you were either cold or hot. So, because you are lukewarm, neither hot nor cold, I will spit you out of my mouth" (Rev 3:15-16).

God finds the lukewarmness of a person unacceptable. It is something repulsive that He cannot tolerate within you. For that reason, sooner or later, He has to lead you to the desert. The circumstances in the desert polarize one's attitudes and cause one to become either hot or cold and no longer lukewarm. Moses, the great saint of the Old Testament, and others, were sanctified in the desert, whereas some people became murderers, criminals, and idolaters. The Fathers of the Church claim that God leads a person to the desert in order for him to believe or to blaspheme; **either faith or blasphemy, but not indifference.** That is how it was in the biblical desert. Many blasphemed against God, and others were sanctified. The gift of the desert does not allow one to maintain the masked attitude of atheism.

The experience of the desert will allow you to understand how senseless the judgment of one person toward another is. This will help you to fight against all of your judgments toward others. What do you know, anyway, about another person whom you meet on your path and in whom you may see a great deal of evil? It is his existential situation that is of prime importance. He could be experiencing trials or he could be in the desert stage. Thus you must not judge others.

The desert is a place of advantage for Satan since then a person is weak and easily succumbs to temptation. Satan takes advantage of this situation. The desert can also, in this way, increase the possibility of rebellion. There were particularly strong temptations and revolts in the desert that the Chosen People crossed. Dramatic situations arose resulting in leaders turning away from God, even to the point of starting the cult of the golden calf.

A person is transformed in the desert; he becomes different since a true polarization of attitudes is brought about. He therefore becomes either better or worse. A person can become a criminal, but he can also become a saint.

THE DESERT: A PLACE OF DENUDATION

The biblical symbolism of the desert is closely connected to God's call for the Chosen People to leave Egypt and to enter the Promised Land. The road from Egypt to Canaan is about four hundred kilometers long. Even a caravan numbering in the thousands could cross that desert in two or three weeks. And yet the journey of the Chosen People lasted forty years. God, by calling His people into the desert, forced them to rid themselves of self-assurance and to submit to a hard life. God called them to submit to the **process of denudation – being** stripped of supports and attachments – which is necessary on the road to faith and to total abandonment to God.

The desert is primarily a **symbol of denudation**. Man stands before the limitless sky, the limitless sand, and before himself. Everything is reduced to the primary and essential elements – open space, the sky, the earth, sand, God and man himself. Entering the desert means being stripped of basic things, and being tormented by hunger and thirst both physically and spiritually. Denudation gives rise to physical and spiritual hunger and thirst, which are inseparable from each other. In these difficulties, that which has been deeply hidden within a person is brought to the surface.

The desert is the place and time for separating oneself from attachments – from one's own systems of security. A person wandering in the desert has nothing. His life's situation is uncertain; he has no securities; he lacks everything. He who crosses the desert experiences the necessity of being satisfied with what he receives from God, and the necessity for awaiting everything from Him. He experiences the necessity of relying solely on God because **God wants to become everything for the traveler through the desert.**

The wandering nation, which received the miraculous manna from God, could not collect more than it needed for a day. The people had to believe anew each day that the manna would fall. They had to believe that God would continuously take care of them. **The desert, therefore, is a place where faith is born. Faith deepens to the extent of denudation.** God will fill a person with His presence to the extent that the person denudes himself and desires to answer God's call, thus opening himself to the love he experiences.

The more a person allows himself to be stripped of his own self and of his own securities, the more God can descend into him and be the only One for him to rely on. **God reminds us that the more this mutual, mysterious relationship between Him and ourselves deepens, the greater becomes the need for our denudation,** which is a way of God fervently calling us to make a more complete gift of ourselves to Him. God expects that the one who loves Him will want to go beyond his human capabilities. He will agree to be totally stripped of all that he is and of all that he possesses, so that he may become a sign, so that God can become a living Presence in the world through him.

The desert is a birthplace of faith that becomes ever more dynamic. This kind of faith transforms a person's life. In the desert, God expects a lukewarm person of little faith to become zealous in faith and self-surrender to the Lord. It was because of the denudation of the people in the desert that the Covenant was made there and that the vows between Israel and God were made. Then God became a gift for the people, and the people promised their gift of faithfulness to God.

THE DESERT: AN EXPERIENCE OF GOD'S LOVE

The denudation which a person experiences in the desert, together with knowing the truth about himself, allows him to come to know the truth about God who is Love. The desert enables him to experience God's presence and power in a special way. Above all, it allows him to experience His mercy.

God responds to sin and to human weakness with love and fatherly concern. To people who rebel and sin, He responds with the miracles of manna and water so desperately needed by them. Despite the human evil, which manifests itself more clearly in the desert, God is present there in a special way. He led the Chosen People. God was visible, while at the same time hidden, in a column of cloud and in a column of fire. The column of cloud that indicated the presence of God, at the same time, hid Him. For the Israelites, the column of cloud was both light and darkness; it symbolized that God was close to them, and yet unreachable.

God led an unorganized crowd into the desert. However, those who crossed it were already a nation united with God through the Covenant; they were a transformed people. The purpose of a desert is the formation of a person by strengthening his faith, eliminating mediocrity, and forming a true disciple of Christ. The Chosen People entered the Promised Land as a small community, but one rich in the experience of the desert. They experienced God amid threatening situations like violent storms with thunder and lightening while, at the same time, experiencing their own weakness and their own failure. They experienced with unusual clarity their own wretchedness, and that is why they experienced God's mercy so greatly.

In the desert you come to know God who never abandons you. It is true that God hides Himself in the desert, but in reality He is very close to you. God is never closer to you than He is then. He only waits for your faith. He waits for you to stretch out your arms to Him in faith.

The Chosen People discovered in their own weakness the true mystery of God. **If you experience your weakness, then you are called by God to throw yourself into His merciful arms.** You experience the desert in your life so that you will turn toward the One who is Mercy Himself.

Experiencing the desert will help you to discover the need for God, and to know that you are completely dependent on Him. During this time, when you go through very difficult hours of discouragement, temptation, and darkness, you will better understand your own helplessness and powerlessness. When you discover the truth about yourself and ask God for forgiveness, you will find, just as the Prodigal Son did, great tenderness in the Father and His extreme joy upon your return. You will be able to look into His eyes full of love. In forgiving you, God will, at the same time, bring about humility within you.

The desert is not a dwelling place; it **is only a path, a road on which one comes to know the merciful love of God.** Everyone who seeks God must pass through it since the experience of the desert is closely related to the deepening of our faith in His mercy.

A desert experience is a time when a person becomes formed according to the rule that only what is difficult and gives resistance molds a person. The love of God, which is then born in you, should finally become communion with God. St. John of the Cross states, "For to love is to labor to divest and deprive oneself for God of all that is not God."[38] **The desert** is not only a place where our faith is born, but it

---

[38] John of the Cross, *The Ascent of Mount Carmel*, 165.

ultimately **becomes the birthplace and dwelling place of our contemplation.**

Going through the desert in your life **you will always meet Mary.** She will be close to you, and will look at you with motherly tenderness and concern. The one who is the Mediatrix of graces and the Mediatrix of mercy will intercede for you with God. She will look at you anxiously to see whether you follow her example and say your *fiat*, your *yes*, and whether you see God in the situations that you experience. The Chosen People did not have Mary with them. She is with you; that is why you will never walk alone. The one who experienced so many difficult situations will walk before you. She will be your light and will show you the road to her Son. Her presence will shine in the darkness of your desert.

Chapter Nine

Rich and Humble
Temporal Means
within the Church

J acques Maritain divides temporal means that may be used for spiritual ends into two categories: *rich temporal means* and *humble temporal means.*[39] Those means which are visible and can be statistically analyzed Maritain calls rich means. They are tangible things like organizations, meetings, marches, church architecture and decoration, audio-visual and mass media. A characteristic trait of rich means is their influence on one's self-love because their effects and results are apparent. This has the danger of our claiming these results as our own and, as a result, adopting an attitude of triumph.

---

[39] Jacques Maritain, *On the Philosophy of History*, (New York: Charles Scribner's Sons, 1957), 70 (italics added by author).

According to Maritain, the second type of means are humble means. They are marked with the stigma of the Cross and express one of the most profound truths in the Gospel: "Unless a grain of wheat falls to the ground and dies, it remains just a grain of wheat; but if it dies, it produces much fruit" (Jn 12:24). In humble means, a true paradox of the dynamism of faith can be observed: the poorer they are – that is, the more destitute, the more insignificant in themselves, and the less visible – the more efficacious they are. As opposed to rich means, these humble means are not dependent on tangible success, and they do not have any internal need for temporal success.

THE POVERTY OF JESUS

In our lives and in the Church we are used to relying on rich means. We very much desire to see the victory and triumph of Christ, and to see His might and authority. Meanwhile, He is hidden; He is poor in Bethlehem, even poorer on Mount Calvary, and maybe He is poorest of all in the Eucharist. By going to such an extreme in His poverty and humility, He emphasizes the importance of humble means.

Jesus chooses poor and humble means, above all, in His redeeming works. No evidence of power is present at His birth. He comes to us as a small child, completely dependent on the people around Him. He resists no one. He can neither do what He wants nor defend Himself. Above all, He lets Himself be known through his lowliness, humility, and weakness. **This is how He appears at the moment of His birth, and this is how He is in His Passion.** He shows that you too must be stripped of everything. He shows that you must die to yourself like a grain of wheat, and choose what is most effective: the humble means.

This does not mean that Jesus did not use rich means. The triumphant arrival into Jerusalem was certainly a rich means; it was the triumph of Christ. Jesus wanted to show that, if He so wished, crowds would give Him great homage and would lay their cloaks before Him. By this He wanted to show that He could do anything. But this event could have misled the apostles. In order for the apostles to remain sober in their thoughts, on Palm Sunday right after His triumphant arrival into Jerusalem, Jesus said the following shocking words, "Amen, amen, I say to you, unless a grain of wheat falls to the ground and dies, it remains just a grain of wheat; but if it dies, it produces much fruit" (Jn 12:24).

There were miracles in the life of Jesus, such as the Transfiguration on Mount Tabor, but above all He used humble means. During His arrest, we once again see rich means used by Him; upon hearing His words the guards had to fall on their faces before Him (cf. Jn 18:6). He threw them to the ground and showed them His power and might. Later, however, He allowed them to ridicule and scorn Him. He allowed them to spit on Him, and to shout at Him on the Cross, "Aha! You who would destroy the temple and rebuild it in three days, save yourself by coming down from the Cross...He saved others; he cannot save himself" (Mk 15:29-31). Jesus, with all His Divine calmness accepted all of this and took up these humble means to save the world.

THE EFFICACY OF HUMBLE MEANS

Humble means is the acceptance of suffering out of love for God. You encounter such means when your knees hurt during prayer, when you deny yourself something, when you question who you are and, at times, live in great calmness, silence, and contemplation. Nothing much is known about these things; they are invisible means. They cannot be measured by any sociological statistics. However, these are the humble means that, in the light of faith, prove to be the deciding factor in the fate of the world.

Rich means are the ones that are valued in the eyes of the world, but they are seen differently in the light of faith. "For the foolishness of God is wiser than human wisdom," St. Paul says, "and the weakness of God is stronger than human strength" (1 Cor 1:25). What is humble in the eyes of people is rich in the eyes of God. **Therefore, humble means are the richest. They are the most effective. They are an indication of true wisdom, the wisdom of the Gospel.** The use of rich means will only be effective when rooted in humble means – in a deep spiritual life, in a life of prayer, in dying to oneself, and in total devotion to God. The efficacy of humble means stems from the presence of Christ in the soul, according to the rule that God is devoted to the soul to the extent that it is devoted to Him. St. Thomas Aquinas says that the works of an active life are born of the fullness of contemplation.[40] The efficacy of rich means (the legalistic-organizational apostolate) flows from the richness of humble means, and not the other way around. Rich

---

[40] *Summa theologica*, 2, 2, qu. 188.

means can be limited by external factors, for example by the lack of time, physical strength, organizational management, or by persecution of the Church. Humble means cannot be taken from the Church by outside factors. Their lack cannot be justified because to make use of them one needs only good will and love.

Rich means are also necessary to the Church and they should not be rejected. God does not want one-sidedness of the apostleship. For example, He wants a Catholic press and a variety of visible forms of this apostolate to exist. St. Maximillian Kolbe is, in a certain sense, a patron of rich means. He dreamed about seeing a million magazines of *"Rycerz Niepokalanej"* (Knight of the Immaculate) go out into the world – and his dream came true. It was Father Kolbe who gave out miraculous medals of the Immaculate in the streets of Japanese cities. He dreamed about a radio station, about planes and ships in the service of the Immaculate. These rich means should not be disregarded and should also be employed in service to the Lord. We have to remember, however, that **their efficacy flows from the presence of humble means**.

St. Maximillian, a man of success, had many things turn out well for him. He founded a large apostolic Marian center named *Niepokalanów* (Town of the Immaculate) near Warsaw, Poland, which became a source of amazement for the entire Church. He founded similar centers of the Immaculate also named *Niepokalanów* on other continents. However, this undoubted success was gained only through humble means. St. Maximillian gave the following testimony about this, "When all other means failed, when they all thought that there was no hope left for me, and my superiors concluded that I was good for nothing, then the 'Immaculate' picked up this instrument, which was only good enough for the rubbish heap."[41] It was Mary, to whom Father Maximillian was totally devoted, who lifted up this little "nothing" in order to make use of him to spread the glory of God and to save souls. The efficacy of his apostleship and his work in the service of the Immaculate began when he became gravely ill. His brothers and superiors then claimed that, because he was in an advanced stage of tuberculosis he was no longer fit to work, and they all had their doubts about him. He was stripped of everything, like the grain of wheat that must die in order to bear fruit. This is a divine paradox. A man who was considered useless in human terms became a most effective instrument in God's hands because **it was God who lived in him and acted through him. It was God who achieved success through this saint.**

Faith is the acknowledgement of one's own helplessness and the awaiting of everything from God. **This experience of helplessness and of awaiting everything from God is humble means _par excellence._** Do you see the value of humble means in your life? God certainly does not limit your opportunities of this kind. Who among us does not undergo moments of torment, some particular difficulties or moments of the spiritual desert? Who among us does not have problems with our own selves and with the external conditions of life? All of this cannot be seen, classified, or evaluated. It is so unnoticeable that one cannot find any

---

[41] Maria Winowska, _Szaleniec Niepokalanej_ [The Folly of the Immaculate] (Niepokalanow, Poland: Wydawnictwo OO. Franciszkanow, 1999), 71.–Ed.

statistical data on this subject. Who could possibly know that, at a certain point in your life, you said *yes* to God, *I do want — I want everything that You expect from me.* Who could know that, at a certain point in time, when it was very hard for you, you said through tears that you love Him and always want to love Him? Who knows how many times you vanquished your own self, denied yourself something, and overcame your own will? **These humble means are of the utmost importance to you, to the Church, and to the world; these are the means that summon the might of God.** How many times has God given you the opportunity to take advantage of them? Maybe you wasted these opportunities or refused to accept these priceless gifts from God. Maybe you even resented them and rebelled, while He almost forced them on you and asked you not to refuse that which is so important to the salvation of the world. St. Maximillian Kolbe, who was called God's Beggar, knew well the value of humble means. You must not forget that it is very important for you to accept humiliation with joy. Try to smile in spite of feeling sad and, in spite of your experiences, try to look at the world cheerfully and with faith that love will certainly conquer all. God appreciates everything: the efforts you make when you kneel on a hard floor and your knees hurt very much, when you stand in a crowded church and your legs ache, or when you are tired on a long drive to church in bad weather. He knows all about the humble means that He has given to you for your use, that you can decide in the depth of your heart to accept or reject. It is in your heart that your own fate is determined and the fate of those closest to you. **Since humble means by themselves do not guarantee your reaching your life's goal, the efficacy of humble means** is based on faith; therefore, this efficacy is the evidence that it is God Himself who is acting.

You may say that you pray a great deal for someone who does not believe, for someone's conversion, or for someone's health. But everything depends on how you pray. Sometimes, your one *yes* spoken to God with joy would suffice. This simple, unassuming means can really perform miracles. If you find it hard to accept God's invitation to participate in the saving of souls, think about John Paul II, about his crown of thorns in the form of being viciously criticized and his great fatigue especially when traveling so often around the world. Think about St. Maximillian for whom so many things worked out only as the result of humble means. So often he found it difficult to breathe, especially during his travels when he was actually suffocating. He writes in his letters that sometimes he simply could not breathe and was totally exhausted. His devotion to the Immaculate was called a folly, but it was his determination in using humble means that was the true folly.

If you have not understood the value of humble means, then you do not understand the depth of Christianity at all. If you do not understand the value and sense of humble means, then you do not understand the Cross that, of course, is at the center of the Church. It was from the Cross that Jesus drew everything to Himself. It was under this Cross that His mother stood and did not take back her *yes* when faced with the terrible suffering of the Savior. It is from the Cross that God's grace of redemption and sanctification of the world flows continuously. The Savior draws you to Himself, not by His triumphant entrance to Jerusalem, but by the Cross. It is from the Cross that He calls you to follow Him and to love Him as He has loved you, "to the end."

The patroness of humble means is Mary who, if judged from the human perspective, did not accomplish any great deed in her lifetime. There were no rich means in her life at all; there was poverty, silence, a hidden life, humility, obedience, prayer, contemplation, and devotion to God. Her life, filled with simplicity and the use of humble means, was a life **hidden in God**. She invites you also to this kind of life. She wants you to live a life of faith, so that in your heart you will desire to use humble means, thus imitating her life in Nazareth. She wants you to see the truth of this statement of St. John of the Cross: "For a little of this pure love is more precious to God and the soul and more beneficial to the Church...than all these other works put together."[42]

VICTORY THROUGH FAITH

The battle with the Amelekites is the classic biblical scene that shows the value and sense of humble means in the light of faith. While crossing the desert on the road to the Promised Land, the Israelites engaged in battle with the Amelekites because the Amelekites controlled the routes through the desert (cf. Ex 17:8-13). Moses, a man of God, knew how to guarantee a victory for his troops. If he were a strategist who thought only in human terms, according to the rules of military strategy, he would have stood at the head of his troops. If he had taken leadership himself, he surely

---

[42] *The Spiritual Canticle*, stanza 29, no.2 in *The Collected Works of St. John of the Cross* (Washington, DC 1991), 587.

would have encouraged his troops since they were so devoted to him. However, he did something that was absurd from the point of view of military strategy. He retreated and left his army under the control of Joshua, his second in command. Then he climbed to the top of the hill to pray there. Moses, as a man of God and a man of prayer, knew very well who decides the fate of the world and the fate of his nation. This is why Moses stood on the top of the hill with his arms outstretched in a gesture of faith. There was a close connection between him and the valley where the battle was raging. When his arms tired, his army retreated. He knew what this meant; **God wanted him to always put forth an effort, to continuously stretch out his arms to the Lord.** Aaron and Hur, who accompanied Moses, supported his arms when they became completely numb. So it was that this gesture of outstretched arms to God, throughout the entire day, accompanied the Israelites in battle. Finally, when night came, victory was theirs. However, it was not Joshua or his army that fought in the valley who were victorious. In fact, it was Moses praying on the hill who was victorious. It was his faith that was victorious.

If this scene were to take place in our time, the attention of the journalists, the television cameras, and the spotlights would be directed toward the place where Joshua was fighting. For us this would be the place where everything would be decided. Who among us would have paid attention to a single praying man? **But it was this single man who was victorious because God was victorious through his faith.**

Moses' outstretched arms are a symbol that it is God who decides everything. He who rules is there; everything depends on Him. Human capabilities can be ridiculously small, but for the Lord nothing is impossible to achieve. **The gesture of outstretched arms, those numbed arms, is a gesture of faith. It is a humble means that expresses the folly of faith in the infinite might and boundless love of the Lord.**

SPIRITUAL MOTHERHOOD

Spiritual motherhood is realized through humble means because it is actualized by participating in Christ's death: "Unless a grain of wheat falls to the ground and dies, it remains just a grain of wheat;" and in His Resurrection: "but if it dies, it produces much fruit" (Jn 12:24). Before all else, sharing in Christ's death is achieved through the acceptance of suffering since it inflicts death on egoism; and participating in the Resurrection is putting on "the new self, created in God's way" (Eph 4:24), in the image of Christ who is Love. It is the apostleship of begetting Christ in souls. It means that the apostle shares Christ who is present in his soul. According to St. Paul, the apostolate is a spiritual fatherhood that, in essence, is the same as spiritual motherhood: "For I became your father in Christ Jesus through the gospel" (1 Cor 4:15). Our apostleship as a spiritual motherhood is, due to faith, a participation in the spiritual motherhood of the Church. **Through our faith, which fully manifests itself by the use of humble means, souls are reborn to live for Christ.** Spiritual motherhood is brought about through the living word that is the fruit of contemplative contact with God. It is brought about through prayerful devotion to God and, in particular, through sacrifice and suffering.

Two great sinners played a special role in the life of St. Thérèse of the Child Jesus. When she was fourteen she learned about one of them, Pranzini, who had murdered three people. Despite being sentenced to death, he showed no remorse. Thérèse could not come to terms with the thought that he might die without being reconciled with God. For a month and a half, she offered all of her prayers and suffering for Pranzini. Then God gave her a sign: this great sinner, in the last moment before his death, took a Crucifix and kissed the wounds of the Savior three times. When Thérèse learned about this, full of emotion, she said to Celine, "**This is my first son.**" Thérèse, being only fourteen, already had such a clear understanding of spiritual motherhood. Later she wrote, "Suffering alone can give birth to souls for Jesus."[43] Pranzini was a prototype of all sinners, whom Thérèse wanted to pray for in a special way and for whom she wanted to offer her suffering. She knew that prayer alone was not enough, that, in order to save souls, one has to offer the greatest gift to God: one's own suffering.

A more dramatic figure of a great sinner, according to the testimonies of St. Thérèse, was Fr. Hyacinthe Loyson. His name is never mentioned in her autobiography, in Thérèse's letters, or in *Story of a Soul*. Only twice in her letters to Celine does she mention, "he is really culpable" and "a certain Lily faded and withered."[44] We find out about her desire to save this soul from the records of the process of beatification and canonization. Hyacinthe Loyson, a Discalced Carmelite, superior of the convent in Paris, was a

---

[43] Thérèse to Celine, LT 129, July 8, 1891 in *Letters of Thérèse of Lisieux*, 2:728.
[44] Ibid.; Thérèse to Celine, LT 127, April 26, 1891 in *Letters of Thérèse*, 2:725.

great and unusually gifted preacher whose conferences moved audiences in all of France. Even the Pope congratulated him on his successes. But, at certain point in time, this exceptionally religious man turned from being a great preacher into becoming an apostate – a fighting apostate. He traveled across the dioceses in France and, despite many protestations, preached that the Church had moved away from the true Gospel. He fought the Church in this way for forty-three years. This battle terrified the convent in Lisieux, so much so that no one had the courage to mention his name. He was never directly mentioned, and that is why his name never appears in the writings of St. Thérèse, who offered her prayers and sufferings for him for nine years. For Pranzini, a month and a half was enough for his conversion, whereas for Fr. Loyson, nine years seemed to be insufficient. Father Loyson was excommunicated, and later wrote an open letter incriminating the Church and the Carmelite Order. This provoked vehement protests and great indignation. Thérèse, however, did not lose hope. With great emotion she said to Celine that his conversion was her main desire. "Dear Celine, he is really culpable, more culpable than any other sinner who was ever converted. But cannot Jesus do once what He has not yet ever done? And, if He were not to desire it, would He have placed in the heart of His poor little spouses a desire that He could not realize?" [45] This is her often-repeated statement: if Jesus gives us the desire for something, then it is not meant to remain unfulfilled. "No, it is certain," she writes, "that He

---

[45] Thérèse to Celine, LT 129, July 8, 1891 in *Letters of Thérèse*, 2:728.

desires more than we do to bring back this poor stray sheep to the fold. A day will come when He will open his eyes."[46]

When we analyze St. Thérèse's faith, we see that her faith was a certainty. She knew that Hyacinthe Loyson would be converted. She wrote, "Let us not grow tired of prayer; confidence works miracles... It is not our merits but those of our Spouse, which are *ours*, that we offer to Our Father who is in heaven, in order that our brother, a son of the Blessed Virgin, return vanquished to throw himself beneath the mantle of the most merciful of Mothers."[47] Thérèse so desired to save his soul that she offered her last Holy Communion for his intention. She died fully realizing that Fr. Hyacinthe Loyson was not converted, but the certainty of her faith remained unshaken. The priest did die fifteen years later at age eighty-five. Jesus loved Thérèse so much that this time He did not have to give her any sign. Jesus knew that she would not stop believing that Fr. Loyson would be converted. When, in 1912, Loyson was dying, there was no Catholic priest with him and there was no confession. It is known, however, that before his death he received a copy of a *Story of a Soul* and read the writings of St. Thérèse in one reading, which he described as "a folly and something quite shocking." During his difficult death, those close to him heard him whisper the words, "Oh, my sweet Jesus."[48] This last act of love directed toward Jesus allows us to assume that Fr. Hyacinthe was saved – thanks to the prayers and sufferings of Thérèse. He was also her spiritual son.

---

[46] Ibid.
[47] Ibid., 729.
[48] LT *129* in *Letters of Thérèse*, endnote no. 6, 2:731

The statement by St. Thérèse that "suffering alone can give birth to souls for Jesus"[49] shows us what spiritual motherhood consists in. A mother is one who gives life and who supports that life. A person fears suffering, but none of us can free ourselves from it, just as we cannot free ourselves from the burden of each day. However, the advantage of our suffering and difficulties can be wasted. Only by accepting them and linking them with the Cross of Jesus will they allow us to enter the extraordinary mystery of spiritual motherhood. **Taking part in the royal priesthood of the faithful, we are called to this kind of motherhood. We are to gain and give birth to souls for Jesus.** Think about all the many things that are difficult for you: maybe poor health, domestic conflicts, rebellious children or some spiritual torment. These things could be even more insignificant but, if they are accepted and offered, they cause you to participate in the spiritual motherhood of the Church, which means giving birth to souls for Christ. **There is nothing more important than this.** This motherhood can be brought about by a verbal apostolate and by an apostolate of prayer. However, suffering is the most effective means. Moreover, it is the most effective form of apostleship, since the greatest nakedness, which is a humble means, is found in suffering. In suffering, the Cross is outstretched the most.

THE TESTIMONY OF JOHN PAUL II

On May 25, 1985, in St. Peter's Square in Rome, Pope John Paul II placed a cardinal's biretta on the head of Archbishop

---

[49] Thérèse to Celine, July 8, 1891 in Thérèse to Celine, LT 129, July 8, 1891 in *Letters of Thérèse*, 2:728.

Andrzej Maria Deskur. This was an unusual consistory that invoked shock and amazement. Why was the Pope appointing a paralyzed man as Cardinal? Surely the dignity of the rank of a cardinal is not a title or reward for the work of a bishop. Cardinals are the first advisers and associates of the Pope. They have a very important role in the Church. Why then was a man who was unable to work because of his suffering appointed a Cardinal? John Paul II discreetly revealed this mystery in the evening of the consistory in his speech to pilgrims from Poland. This is what he said about Cardinal Deskur, "He is particularly close to me from long ago, in my student years in the seminary, throughout the years of my priesthood and through many meetings in Rome, but especially throughout the last meeting before the conclave. Then the Providence of God touched Bishop Deskur with this extreme handicap, which he has until today. Among all the cardinals appointed today, he is the only one in a wheelchair and brings into this College of Cardinals a special stigma, the stigma of suffering which is a sacrifice. We do not know the ways of God; we do not know God's mysteries, but it is hard for me, personally, not to be convinced that the sacrifice of Archbishop, now Cardinal Andrzej, happened in connection with the conclave which took place in the middle of October, 1978." In the suffering of Archbishop Andrzej Deskur, the Holy Father saw the price that was paid so that he, Cardinal Wojtyla, could become the successor of Christ. We know that as soon as the Pope was elected, his first steps were directed toward the Gemelli clinic where the sick and paralyzed Archbishop Andrzej Maria Deskur lay. He was the one to whom the Pope, according to his own opinion, owed so much. The Pope went to meet the one who had given the

Pope the better part – his help through suffering, a difficult part, but the most effective like all humble means. The fact that the disabled Archbishop Andrzej Maria Deskur was appointed Cardinal is an indirect indication by John Paul II of the value of humble means.

Cardinal Deskur was previously the head of the Papal Commission for Mass Media. Thus he was in charge of the distribution and function of rich means within the Church. He did much in this field. He contributed a great deal toward preparing the documents of the Church, which laid out the way of action for the Catholic Mass Media. However, the Pope did not mention these merits. He said nothing about the greatness of Cardinal Deskur's contribution for the development of the Mass Media. The Cardinal brought with him into the College of Cardinals the stigma of suffering, which is a sacrifice. One gets the impression that, in this way, the Pope wanted to emphasize the value of humble means.

On the first of June in the afternoon, Cardinal Andrzej Maria Deskur received his titular Church of San Cesareo in Palatio, the same church that was received by Cardinal Karol Wojtyla in 1967. The Cardinal, in the majesty of his suffering, celebrated Mass seated. Instead of a cardinal's throne, there stood an armchair on wheels by a low altar. His hand, crippled by the illness, held the crosier with difficulty. This was a peculiar paradox: the head of the Papal Commission in matters of rich means was marked by the stigma of humble means.

The words of John Paul II regarding the attempt on his life should also be understood in the context of the doctrine of humble means. He called that incident a particular grace. On October 14, 1981, during the Wednesday general audience in St. Peter's Square, while speaking to thousands of pilgrims, he said these significant words: "God allowed me to experience suffering through the past months, allowed me to experience my life in peril, and allowed me at the same time to understand clearly and profoundly that this is His special grace for myself as a person. It is a grace for the Church as well since I serve as the successor of St. Peter. Christ gave me this grace that I may give testimony of His love through suffering and through the danger to my life and health. I find this to be a particular grace and for this I offer special thanksgiving to the Holy Spirit and to the Immaculate Virgin Mary."

Without humble means, without the suffering that marked his life, could John Paul II have so effectively been the shepherd of the Church? Could he have drawn crowds? The Pope mentions the dramatic days of the attempt on his life once more on his saint's feast day, November 4, 1981: "The incident on the thirteenth of May gave me a great deal to think about and made me look even more, in the light of the Gospel, at my human and Christian life according to those words about the grain that must die so that it can bear fruit."

PART THREE

THE ACTUALIZATION OF FAITH

F aith should permeate our entire life. Thanks to faith, the believer enters with all his humanity and all of his ordinary everyday life into an intimate relationship with God. Faith is most fully actualized through the sacraments, especially through the sacraments of Christian initiation. It is because of faith that we can see and accept the redeeming works of Christ in those sacraments. **Baptism** is the first sacrament of Christian initiation. In this sacrament we receive the gift of faith together with the gift of supernatural life. In a baptized person a fundamental consecration is brought about through incorporation into Christ. This consecration means that a person is offered to God and is called to holiness. **Confirmation**, as the second sacrament of Christian initiation, intensifies the dynamism of faith, enriches the baptized with a special strength of the Holy Spirit, and emphasizes his responsibility for spreading and defending the faith. Moreover, through the **Eucharist**, which is the sacrament of the culmination of our faith and the third sacrament of initiation, we can be intimately united with the crucified and risen Christ. Partaking in the Redemptive Sacrifice of Christ is the summit of life in faith. United with the sacrifice of Christ, we offer ourselves to God the Father. The Eucharist creates a community of faith in which we together make our offering and are united with Christ.

Faith is being actualized through prayer in a particular way since **prayer**, which is initiated and developed through faith, is the dialogue between man and God the Father through Jesus Christ in the Holy Spirit. Faith is also brought about by **listening intently to the Word of God**, which is a form of dialogue with Him. In this dialogue a person willingly entrusts himself to God. A person shows compliance of intellect and will by obedience in faith to God, who then reveals Himself. It is also necessary for faith to be expressed in deeds of **love** without which it is dead. Faith, as a permanent process of being converted, is an incessant opening of oneself to the love of God and is the continual acceptance of this love so that it can be bestowed on others.

CHAPTER TEN

THE SACRAMENT OF BAPTISM

B aptism is a summit of the actualization of faith, as are the other sacraments. Baptism is the foundation and the beginning of this process of actualization; it is a beginning directed toward the fullness of life in Christ.[50] In conciliar thought, the sacrament of Baptism is called a sacrament of faith, as are all the other sacraments. All the sacraments require faith, presume that faith is present, and are a sign of faith, while at the same time, allow faith to grow. Faith precedes Baptism and leads to it. Faith is the disposition of the soul to receive Baptism.

Through Baptism, death to sin is brought about in us. This is a real death, the destruction in a person of that which

---

[50] Second Vatican Council, *Unitatis Redintegratio* (Decree on Ecumenism), no. 22 [Proclaimed by Pope Paul VI on November 21, 1964].

was evil and unredeemed **so that he may be reborn as a son of God, becoming a new creature, a partaker in the divine nature, who is called to holiness.**[51] Through Baptism, a person is offered and consecrated to God; he becomes His true worshiper and His adopted child. When speaking about Baptism, the Second Vatican Council reveals truths to us that are beyond the human intellect and imagination. It speaks of our incorporation into the crucified and glorified Christ and of conforming ourselves to His image. It says that through Baptism man receives the gift of faith and from then on partakes in the royal priesthood of Christ. Through this he becomes a partaker in His priestly, prophetic, and royal ministry and is incorporated, although not yet completely, into His Mystical Body.

IMMERSION INTO THE DEATH AND RESURRECTION OF CHRIST

Because of our little faith, Baptism remains the sacrament not yet fully appreciated by Christians. Deep faith is needed to understand the words of St. Paul: "For you have died, and your life is hidden with Christ in God" (Col 3:3). Paul's expression "have died" has the same meaning as the words used by the apostle in his letter to the Romans when he writes about the importance of the sacrament of Baptism leading us into the life of Christ: "Or are you unaware that we who are baptized in Christ were baptized into his death?" (Rom 6:3). It is a consequence of His death that we enter a new life through Baptism. This first sacrament of the Church

---

[51] Cf. *LG*, no. 40.

is the beginning of our being "hidden with Christ in God." **Baptism is the origin and source of faith.** It begins a supernatural life in us, which is a life of faith, hope, and love.

From this point on, we are buried with Christ for sin, for moral evil, and for everything that is not Christ-like. This is a true death because all attachments to the world and to any other value besides God must die within us so that we may enter a new life, which began in the Resurrection of Christ.

In every religious system, the phenomenon of double birth occurs. A person is born, not only in the physical sense, but also in the spiritual sense. Birth in a spiritual sense is a kind of initiation. In certain non-Christian religions, these initiations have developed into extremely dramatic forms based on the symbolism of death and rebirth. These forms are dramatic because their symbolism takes advantage of what terrifies one in death and of what is considered wonderful in a new life. Many of these dramatized forms revert to strong symbolism and images, such as being buried in the ground, being thrown through an opening surrounded by burning torches, being devoured by a mythical monster, or actually being buried with a dead body. This is all done to shake someone up and to cause emotional shock, which deeply affects the human imagination. In the non-Christian systems, the initiation is based only on the imagination, since it can only attract the imagination.

In Christianity, initiation, understood as a birth into a supernatural life, is brought about by three sacraments: Baptism, Confirmation, and the Eucharist. The symbolism and sacramental signs in these sacraments relate to faith and not to the imagination. It would be inadequate to relate the sacraments to the imagination since the denotation of sacramental signs is beyond all human thought and imagination.

Through Baptism it is as if a new, supernatural organism is grafted into human nature. A new life is grafted into one's life. If a scientist were able to successfully transplant animal life into something that previously had only a vegetative life (for example, a plant), the world would be greatly amazed. Observing an experiment such as this, people would be shocked when they perceive that a plant begins to see, hear, feel, and react to sound. It would most certainly be declared the greatest miracle of human genius. Meanwhile, this transplantation brought about in the sacrament of Baptism is, beyond all imagination, much more significant than the above mentioned fictional transplantation of a new type of life.

When we observe the sacramental signs of water being poured on an infant or adult catechumen's head, the anointing of the head with the sacred chrism, and the giving of the candle and white garment, these signs are not able to reveal to us the reality of what is being brought about. A person is not capable of fathoming it without faith. **Only living faith allows us to see the redeeming action of Christ in Baptism and to accept it.**

Baptism allows us to share in the absolutely new life that Christ began in the history of mankind through His Resurrection. This newness of life is our freedom from the legacy of sin, from its "enslavement," and is our sanctification in truth. **It is the discovering of God's call to be united with Him and to live with Christ in Him.** This newness has within itself the beginnings of all human vocations. Ultimately every call, be it a call to the priesthood or religious life, or to fatherhood or motherhood, leads toward the full actualization of the sacrament of Baptism.

Dying with Christ, which is initiated at Baptism, allows us to partake in the fruits of His Resurrection, like the seed that must die in order to bear fruit that is new life. **Through Baptism a fundamental consecration is brought about, the offering of a human being to God to belong only to Him.** This consecration can be brought about thanks to the graces of Christ's Redemption, and, at the same time, it is our answer to it.

We should continually return to the grace of the sacrament of Baptism so that, through our faithfulness to these extraordinary and particular graces, we may achieve to a degree the state of purity of our soul as was given to us at the moment of Baptismal initiation. By immersion into the death and Resurrection of Jesus through Baptism, we achieve a certain state of immaculateness, which we often waste later. The graces of Baptism are given to us for a lifetime. Nevertheless, we often squander them by submitting to evil. However, if we desire to progress toward sanctity, then by going through various stages of purification, we can once again reach this particular state of immaculateness that we have wasted by being unfaithful to the graces of Baptism. Our whole path to sanctity is nothing other than achieving the same state of our soul that we received at the moment of Baptism.

Progress in our interior life depends on an ever stronger desire to actualize the graces of Baptism – graces of being molded into the image of Christ by living in the spirit of the eight Beatitudes: "Whoever loses his life for my sake will find it" (Mt 16:25). This "losing of one's life" begins with the sacrament of Baptism and is to be actualized throughout a person's entire life. We should lose our life for the sake of Christ by trying to imitate Him ever more fully on the path of our life according to His will and His plan for us. We have to be "buried" with Christ. Because of this, we must go through our own death. That is why, as far as we have not died to everything that separates us from God, our holiness, our life "hidden with Christ in God" (cf. Col 3:3) cannot become a reality. By losing our life for Christ, we respond to the call to find ourselves in Him who is "the whole fullness" (Col 2:9).

The gift of faith given to us in the sacrament of Baptism should lead us to the steady growth of our adherence to Christ.[52] Baptism stands before us not only as something accomplished, but also as a certain mission and purpose. Similar to faith, Baptism is a mission for us that will not be completely fulfilled until the moment of our union with Christ. Then we will be able to repeat the words of St. Paul: "Yet I live, no longer I, but Christ lives in me" (Gal 2:20).

INCORPORATION INTO THE CHURCH AS THE BODY OF CHRIST

An important redemptive consequence of Baptism is the **incorporation of the newly baptized into the community of the Church**. The faith that is born in Baptism causes us to

---

[52] Second Vatican Council, *Gravissimum Educationis* (Declaration on Christian Education), no. 2 [Proclaimed by Pope Paul VI on October 28, 1965].

come out of the seclusion of our own self, and allows us to enter into communion with Jesus, as well as with those who are part of His Mystical Body. The Church becomes the place of our faith. Our faith becomes a part of the Church's faith. If we were separated from the Church, our faith would have no chance of development.

According to the statements of the Second Vatican Council, the Mystical Body of Christ is built by the Christian sacraments of initiation. Through Baptism we are incorporated into it, and subsequently we are strengthened by Confirmation and the Eucharist. However, the perception of our belonging to the Mystical Body of Jesus and our gaining life from this belonging is impossible without living faith.

Very often the people present at a baptism are as if blinded; they look, but they do not see or understand. Unaware that an event is taking place that is beyond our imagination, they are more interested in the child's behavior – focusing on whether he is crying or remaining quiet. If they had faith, they would be amazed because they would realize what a great event is taking place at the moment the water is poured on the head of the person being baptized, as these words are being said, "I baptize you in the name of the Father, and of the Son, and of the Holy Spirit." Only living faith allows you to see past the simple sacramental signs to the inconceivable reality taking place at that time. Lack of faith may lead one to either comprehend somewhat magically the causality of the sacrament of Baptism, or to comprehend it as a purely external function of the Church.

One cannot build or deepen one's personal faith, of which Baptism is the source, only through private dialogue with Jesus, because **faith has the dimension of communion with others**. And in this dimension, faith is also to be born and developed. The sacrament of Baptism is a very important event for the entire parish. Prayers, together with the attitude of faith provided by the local community of the faithful, should accompany the person receiving this first sacrament of the Church. It is through this sacrament that God grants special graces, not only to the newly baptized, but also to the community accepting him. This community is receiving a new, sanctified member. So it is important that in the spirit of deep faith and gratitude we should all accept this great gift of God.

Through the sacrament of Baptism one enters the communion of saints. The grace of Christ, like a powerful river of life, penetrates all who belong to His Mystical Body. The same Holy Spirit acts in everyone. His graces are received not only for oneself, but also for others – spreading these graces through thought, word, and works of love. Growth in grace through a greater faithfulness to God intensifies one's specific influence on others like invisible radiation. This influence is brought about, not only through the spoken or written word, or by giving a good example, but regardless of our direct actions or physical distance. As Romano Guardini has said:

> The prayers of others belong also to you just as their actions, spiritual growth, and purity of heart do. Have you ever reflected on the community of the suffering, on the fact that the graces flowing from somebody's suffering are transferred to others? **If, united with the suffering of Christ, you offer your painful experiences to God for**

others, then your experiences become a living, beneficial, redemptive, power for them. Beyond all obstacles and distances, you bring help where nothing else can be of help. ("Il senso della Chiesa" in *La realtà della Chiesa* [Brescia, Italy: Morcelliana, 1979], p. 38.)

No one is a solitary island. As the Mystical Body of Christ, we constitute a unique network system, similar to a system of connected vessels. Your good as well as your evil has a social dimension, because it creates a specific supernatural pressure of good or evil on others. Prayer, seen in the light of faith, situates itself within a closed system of connected vessels. In such a system, there is never a solitary prayer. As a member of the mystical organism of the Church, you either enrich or impoverish it through your prayer of faith. This determines the ecclesial dimension of prayer and defines your responsibility toward the Church and toward others. It is not the thoughtless saying of prayers, but authentic prayer that, as a form of actualization of faith, reaches God Himself. In order to have an effect on others, prayer does not have to have the character of a clear intercession for someone. It is enough that faith, hope, and charity grow in you at the same time as your prayer life intensifies. The Church and the whole Mystical Body of Jesus will be able to feel the beneficial, saving influence of your prayer.

Within the Mystical Body of Christ, understood in this way, there are mutual bonds of varying degrees of closeness and depth. The physical image of **a system of connected vessels** can enlighten us about the mystery of mutual bonds within the Mystical Body of Christ. A family, as a domestic church, can be an example of a system of connected vessels. Usually God, wanting to affect a particular group of people, uses one of them in a special way so that through that person He can bestow graces on the others. Let us assume, for example, that in a system of connected vessels, such as a family of four, three people are closed to life in grace. They are like hermetically sealed test tubes. If just one of the persons tries to turn toward God, he or she becomes a channel of grace for their loved ones. This person has two possibilities for influencing the others. He can try to remove the stopper from above, just as a corkscrew removes a cork. But if the stopper is made up of live tissue of human personality, forcing access through the top will always bring about suffering, painful and destructive wounds, as well as significant limitation of personal freedom. God does not want this. He loves His children to make decisions in **freedom** of choice, striving for fuller faith and love. Continuing further with the image of connected vessels and sealed test tubes, one can say that God prefers stoppers to be pushed out from below by the specific pressure of grace within your test tube. Before converting others, try first of all to be converted yourself. The greatness of your faith and your adherence to Christ is important. John Paul II said that it is not important what you do, it is important who you are. **The more good there is in you and the more faithfully you follow grace, the more effective your influence on others will be.**

Therefore, if a wife wants to convert her husband who, for example, has a drinking problem, she must begin with her own conversion. It is she who must first be converted. Her spouse may be converted through the basic pressure of goodness increasing within her. This can only be brought about when she grows in grace and deepens her conversion. The reformation of the world and the transformation of others must begin with ourselves. The life of Christ must first increase to such an extent in you that the graces and good accepted by you cause the conversion of others. It can happen that this kind of conversion remains ineffective; that it requires an ever greater "pressure" of grace in your "test tube." This is when God may ask you to lead a more intense spiritual life and even to offer yourself completely to Him, which amounts to a radical striving for sanctity. This is the consequence of your belonging to the Mystical Body of Christ, the consequence of this extraordinary truth, that through Baptism you have become a member of the Total Christ, of His Mystical Body.

G. K. Chesterton wrote that throughout the history of the Church, the Christian faith suffered a seeming death at least five times.[53] One of these dramatic periods, when the Church was dying, was during the time of St. Francis of Assisi. Among documents that give testimony to a very dismal image of the Church in the twelfth century are numerous papal bulls (edicts) written by Pope Innocent III condemning the scandals of usury, venality, gluttony, drunkenness, and debauchery. Together with the decline of morality, many fanatical and aggressive heresies arose in Europe that nearly destroyed Christianity. Another blow to the Church were the wandering preachers who continually criticized the clergy as being often preoccupied with greed for wealth. They preached that the clergy were the opposite of the model of evangelical poverty.

---

[53] *The Everlasting Man* (New York: Image books, 1974), 260.

Francis never criticized anyone. He believed that if evil was all around, it was he, and not others, who must first be converted. If such great abundance of wealth and debauchery was rife, then it was through his fault. It was he who must become radically poor and pure. Saints differ from those who create heresies because heretics want to convert others, but do not want to convert themselves, whereas **saints turn all the cutting edges of criticism toward themselves; they strive to be converted so that the world can be better.**

The more rot and scandal that St. Francis saw around him, the more he desired to conform to the image of Christ in purity, humility, and poverty. It was he, Francis, whose fault it was that the world was so evil; therefore, it was he, Francis, who had to be radically converted – and history proved that he was right. For when Francis was converted, when he became so "transparent" to the Lord that the image of Christ could be reflected in him, Europe then began to heave itself up from its fall. The dream of Pope Innocent III came true. He had dreamed that a figure resembling Francis was supporting the unsteady walls of the Basilica of St. John Lateran – named the "mother and head of all churches" (which is a symbol of the whole Church) – and Francis saved it.

By the power of Francis' sanctity Christ raised His Church from the "death" of its faith. The world was enriched by his sanctity, not so much in the way of learning about a man who actualized the spirit of the Gospel in an extraordinary and heroic way, but in the way of the system of connected vessels, since his sanctity affected people that he never came into contact with. The light of faith lets you see that, through Baptism, you belong to the Body of Christ, that you are incorporated into the system of connected vessels of this Body. This Body so greatly needs the converted and the saints. It is in great need of your conversion and your sanctity. Thanks to the light of faith, you come to know that the reformation of others should always begin with yourself.

Every one of your good deeds affects others. **Your faithfulness is the strength for those whom you love.** When you receive Holy Communion, not only are you strengthened, but also your spouse, children, brother, friends, parish, the Church, and the world. Begin then with yourself, with your own opening up to Christ. God wants you to be sanctified, and through this, He wants to sanctify your environment, your loved ones, the Church, and the world.

THE PRIESTHOOD OF THE FAITHFUL

The common baptismal priesthood of the faithful is most fully expressed in the offering of the Eucharist. Not only does the priest who is celebrating Holy Mass represent Christ-the-Priest, so do the faithful. Together with the priest and through his intercession, they offer the sacrifice of Christ and offer also themselves to God. The Second Vatican Council speaks of this expressly. In Baptism Christ gives to the faithful "a sharing in his priestly function of offering spiritual worship," of offering "the divine victim to God, and [of offering] themselves along with It."[54] "The baptized, by regeneration and the anointing of the Holy Spirit, are consecrated as a spiritual house and a holy priesthood, in order that through all those works which are those of the

---

[54] LG, no. 34; cf. LG, nos. 31, 11.

Christian man they may offer spiritual sacrifices."[55] In the sacrament of the Eucharist, the baptized resemble Jesus Christ in a special way, for not only do they collaborate in the Offertory, but they themselves also become the offertory gift.

The common priesthood of the faithful is connected to the call to offer everything to God, connected with the call to holiness. Your Mass, celebrated within the common priesthood of the faithful, is beneficial when you actually offer yourself to Christ completely and, through Him, fully offer yourself to the Father – when you want nothing for yourself and accept being denuded similar to Christ. **God, who is jealous of your love, desires this total gift.** The priesthood of the faithful should lead you toward a greater engrafting of yourself into Christ. You must, like Christ, be a total gift to the Father reserving nothing for yourself, for only then will He be able to offer Himself fully to you and fill you with Himself.

The increasing presence of Christ in you should be passed on to others. Through Baptism you have been called to *contemplata aliis tradere* – to hand on to others what you are living. Through Baptism you become a member of the prophetic office of Christ. **You are, therefore, called to perform apostolic and evangelizing functions.** St. Peter connects the priesthood of the faithful with the duty of the apostolate and evangelization. You are in the "royal priesthood;" you should announce everywhere your love of Him, who called us out of the darkness into His wonderful light (cf. 1 Pet 2:9).

---

[55] *LG*, no. 10.

John Paul II, in his homily given in Mexico on January 29, 1979, said, "All the faithful, by virtue of their baptism and of the sacrament of confirmation, must publicly profess the faith received from God by means of the Church, spread it and defend it as true witnesses of Christ. That is, they are called to evangelization, which is a fundamental duty of all the members of the people of God." However, you must remember that the efficacy of your apostolic efforts will flow from a deep interior life. It will flow from a life of prayer and total devotion to Christ-the-Priest, by following the example of Mary, whose virginal and total devotion to God became the source of her spiritual motherhood for souls. Baptism, through which you are born into faith, also calls you to such motherhood.

Chapter Eleven

Confirmation

The sacrament of Confirmation is closely related to Baptism and to the Eucharist because it is also a sacrament of Christian initiation. Baptism incorporates the baptized into the Church and Confirmation performs a further, more perfect incorporation into the Body of Christ. The sacrament of Confirmation multiplies the dynamism of graces originating in Baptism and endows us with a special strength of the Holy Spirit. Hence, by the sacrament of Confirmation we are more strictly obliged to be witnesses of Christ, to spread and defend the faith.[56] For people with faith, Confirmation, together with Baptism and the Eucharist, is required for the process of being transformed into the image of Christ to take place and deepen.

In the sacrament of Confirmation we receive the grace of Pentecost, the full outpouring of the Holy Spirit. In its

---

[56] LG, no. 11.

liturgical texts, the Church compares the graces of this sacrament to those extraordinary graces that were granted to the apostles on the day of Pentecost. Confirmation is the solemn "descent" by the Holy Spirit into the baptized. The Holy Spirit desires to bring to maturity what was begun once and forever in Baptism. A special fruit of this sacrament is the **gift of mature faith** given to us by the Holy Spirit.

FULLNESS OF FAITH REQUIRES DENUDATION

Our faith deepens when we are being stripped of our own systems of security, of all that begets feelings of strength, power, and importance in us. Our stripping makes room for faith and demands our humility. By stripping us of our power and strength, God brings us closer to Him, places us in the truth, and causes us to need Him more. This is an extraordinary grace.

St. John of the Cross has said that **God loves a soul most when He strips it,** for one can then achieve **the fullness of faith.** When you have no support from any of your systems of security, then God can attract you to rely solely on Him, the only rock of your salvation. **The grace of denudation is a special gift of the Holy Spirit who, before descending onto a person, strips him.** Often we do not fully understand the work of the Holy Spirit. We know that He is the Power, the Paraclete, and the Love of the Father and the Son; but we often forget that it is **He who is the principal author of our holiness.** Therefore, He is the One who brings about the entire process that is indispensable to us on our path toward unity with God. This process has elements of attraction and elements of purgation. It is the Holy Spirit who denudes us; it is **He who causes us to become poor**. It is He who endows the poor since He is called "Father of the poor," as professed in the hymn of Pentecost.

Does the Holy Spirit endow us in order to make us rich? This would make no sense because, according to the Gospel, being rich in spirit is a curse. **Stripping us** and making us even poorer **is His gift** so that we may be more open to His strength and to His love. Only then will **He Himself become a gift for us**, since then He will be able to descend into the emptiness of our nakedness and fill us with His infinite power and love.

A particularly important kind of denudation by which the Holy Spirit prepares us for His descent is the process of stripping us of the false image we have of ourselves and freeing us from living in falsehood. In the Gospel, St. John relates Christ's promise to us that the Paraclete – the Holy Spirit – will convince the world about sin when He comes (cf. Jn 16:8). This is one of the functions of the Holy Spirit who descends upon us in Confirmation – to convince us of our sin, **to bestow the grace of humility**. This is a fundamental grace of the Holy Spirit. It is because of this grace that we come to know who we really are, and we become convinced that we are sinners and people of little faith.

If you are self-confident – if up until now you have not yet discovered your own sinfulness and are self-sufficient in everything – then, in reality, you do not need the Holy Spirit. Your attitude of self-confidence and your lack of humility close your heart to His descent upon you. If you do not feel that you are a sinner, you will not desire the redeeming action of the Holy Spirit in your life, and then you will not receive the graces of the sacrament of Confirmation. **Humility and faith**, the fundamental gifts of the Holy Spirit, **open us ever more fully to His descent upon us and to acceptance of the Holy Spirit Himself as a gift.**

THE FRUITFULNESS OF THE SACRAMENT OF CONFIRMATION

The graces of a sacrament do not work automatically. Confirmation does not erase the faults in your character, does not eliminate inadequacies in your temperament, and will not substitute for your own efforts. After its reception, you could still remain miserable, fearful, lukewarm in your faith, and a slave to the consideration of what other people think about you. The strength given to you by the Holy Spirit in the sacrament of Confirmation is initially only proposed to you so that you may freely accept it through faith. You can reject this grace and disregard it. The Holy Spirit comes to a person very gently, without imposing Himself, in the silence of the heart that is hungry for His coming. He will come only when you are hungry for Him, when you yearn to hear every word of His and desire His work within your life. The Holy Spirit will come to you depending on the extent of your hunger for His presence and your yearning for His works in your heart.

The path toward maturity of faith is not a regular movement in a straight line. It is usually marked with many ups and downs. In order to reach maturity of faith, you must often experience the faults of your own immaturity. First you must become humble; then you can grow in faith. Growth in humility, which is truth, will enable you to open yourself all the more to the graces of Confirmation and to grow in these graces. After receiving Confirmation you may consider that you have completed a certain stage in your religious life while, in reality, it is the beginning of your journey toward fullness in the life of faith. It is a sacrament that requires your cooperation. Confirmation initiates something extraordinarily important in your life. It initiates a new process of your cooperation with the Holy Spirit who has come to you and is waiting. He is waiting so that, through the growth of your humility and faith, your heart will be completely opened to His descent upon you.

Before receiving the sacrament of Confirmation, during the renewal of the baptismal profession of faith, the Church asks you a question, "Do you believe in the Holy Spirit, Lord and Giver of Life, whom you are to receive today in the sacrament of Confirmation just as the apostles received Him on the day of Pentecost?" In order to answer this question once again, you must stand in the truth before God. When looking at your life in the spirit of humility, which is to remain in the truth, should you not question your faith? How little faith there must be in you if you do not live by the graces of Baptism and by the graces of Confirmation. What has changed in your life since you accepted the fullness of the Holy Spirit? If you were baptized as a baby, you were unaware of the great transformation that Baptism brought about in you, and you were unaware that this was your rebirth. It was your parents and godparents who then professed the faith on your behalf. Later, during Confirmation, you renewed this profession of faith. Were you fully aware at that time that you were choosing Christ, that you wanted to belong to Him completely? While trying to remain in the truth, frequently pose the following questions to yourself: *What have I done with the gifts of the Holy Spirit? What have I done with the Holy Spirit Himself whom I received as an inexpressible gift?*

The validity of the sacrament does not imply its fruitfulness in the person who receives it. A sacrament may be valid but, in spite of this, one may not receive the graces connected with it or, even worse, one may be guilty of unworthy reception of the sacrament. St. Paul, speaking about the Eucharist, warns, "Therefore whoever eats the bread or drinks the cup of the Lord unworthily will have to answer for the body and blood of the Lord" (1 Cor 11:27). The sacraments bestow grace only upon those who do not resist it. The Holy Spirit needs your openness, your internal disposition. He stands at the door and knocks, but He will not enter uninvited. You can, therefore, close yourself to Him, or through faith and humility, you can open the door of your heart wide to Him.

The sacrament of Confirmation received in a state of mortal sin or without faith is valid, but it is dormant and fruitless. However, it can begin to awaken when you are properly disposed. The Holy Spirit descended upon you in the sacrament of Confirmation. If you received this sacrament with little faith, not realizing the importance of this extraordinary event, then you can repair this now by becoming increasingly disposed toward it. The graces of this sacrament should revive and grow in you throughout your entire life until you achieve full unity with Jesus in the Holy Spirit.

THE GIFT OF THE HOLY SPIRIT TO THE APOSTLES

During the Last Supper Jesus said to the apostles, "I have much more to tell you, but you cannot bear it now. But when he comes, the Spirit of truth, he will guide you to all truth" (Jn 16:12-13). On the day before Christ died, the apostles were still unable to accept all of His teachings, since the Holy Spirit had not yet descended on them. Why did the Holy Spirit not descend upon them immediately, at the beginning, when they first met Jesus and followed Him? If this had happened, they would have then fully understood His teachings, whereas up to that point they understood little of what Jesus told them. The Holy Spirit, however, could not descend upon the apostles at the beginning because they did not possess the necessary disposition. They were not yet denuded; they did not have true humility; and they also lacked an authentic faith – a faith that would enable them to remain helpless and to await everything from God.

A person of faith must be stripped of his systems of security. This was very apparent in the lives of the apostles. The process of denudation leads either to rebellion and turning away from God, or to a greater dynamism of faith and a more trustful self-entrustment to God. The rich young man, who with much fervor asked Jesus what he should do to achieve eternal life, ultimately refused to follow the Lord. He did not want to leave everything. That is why, referring to him, Christ said, "It is easier for a camel to pass through [the] eye of [a] needle than for one who is rich to enter the kingdom of God" (Mk 10:25). The apostles were astonished, and Peter's reaction was, Lord, what will happen to us who have given up everything and followed you? (cf. Mk 10:28).

A certain feeling of superiority and satisfaction could have arisen in Peter's soul. He could have said: *That man did not follow the Lord, but we really did leave everything.* No one could contradict this. Peter really did leave his family and his profession, just as John and James did. We know from the Gospel that they left their father Zebedee, who most likely had some kind of fishing business since he employed hired workers and was probably a rich man (cf. Mk 1:16-20). They also left their families, professions, and safeguards; they left everything in order to follow Jesus. However, as it usually happens, a person can be ready to give up everything to God immediately, but later is ready to appropriate everything to himself again.

The apostles, John and James for example, had given up everything for Jesus and later became very self-confident. They had a clear vision of a temporal kingdom of Israel and wanted to make a career for themselves in this kingdom. Moreover, it seems that they were jealous of Peter because he was set apart from the others. Their mother, surely not without their knowledge, asked Jesus that they be seated on His right and left side. Thus one can give up everything only to reclaim everything again later. In their desires, these apostles claimed pre-eminent positions in the kingdom of Jesus for themselves. They really were true Pharisees in their spirit, even though they were not Pharisees formally or nominally. In order to clearly see their Pharisaism, let us recall the situation when Jesus, on His journey to Jerusalem, wanted to pass through a Samaritan city. The inhabitants of this city would not accept Him due to their intolerance toward Jews. It was then that James and John, called the "sons of thunder," said, "Lord, do you want us to call down fire from heaven to consume them?" (Lk 9:54). This is a true characteristic of Pharisaism; regarding themselves as superior, they demand to punish those who in their perception are inferior.

You may leave everything, follow the Lord, and then regard yourself as greater and superior to others; and, by doing this, you accept the poison of Pharisaism. This also happened to the apostles. We see, however, that as long as they were so pharisaical, as long as they claimed so much for themselves, the Holy Spirit could not descend upon them. Surely it would have been easiest for the Holy Spirit, the Paraclete, to descend upon them at the very beginning and explain all the teachings of Jesus. He is the One who sanctifies and makes straight the paths in human souls, and He is the light. However, the **Holy Spirit will not descend into a person rich in spirit,** as Jesus said, "But woe to you who are rich" (Lk 6:24). He cannot descend into a self-confident person who is rich in spirit because this kind of person is not open to the strength of the Holy Spirit who is the **Father of the poor.**

In the lives of the apostles, various stages **of their coming closer to God** can be clearly distinguished. At first, there was a Galilean spring in their lives – joyous and full of dreams. It was not until later that dark clouds began to appear on the horizon. Conflicts with the Pharisees arose, and this gave rise to fear and dread in them. These were the first signs of purgation and the first trials of faith in their lives. Thomas, a witness of the attempts to stone and arrest Jesus, said with resignation and close to despair, "Let us also go to die with him" (Jn 11:16). Then they were no longer the triumphant apostles in their Galilean spring. They started to fear because they were getting closer to a confrontation with the elite of the nation, with the power that, in those times, was wielded by the Pharisees and the Sadducees.

A supreme purification and genuine trial of faith occurred during the Passion of Christ. Good Friday, the day of Jesus' Passion through which the Redemption of the world was brought about, concluded with a night full of purification for the apostles. Then everything fell apart for them; everything collapsed. There was no kingdom; Jesus was defeated; there was no prospect for the future; there was nothing to await and only despair remained. John must have also felt this despair when standing at the foot of the Cross, although the Gospel does not mention this directly. He must have been totally crushed.

Some may say that if you have not gone through a trial of despair then you really do not know anything. The apostles went through this kind of trial of despair on Good Friday. Being Pharisees in spirit, the apostles were then stripped of everything. After the Resurrection, the appearances of the resurrected Christ enlightened that night of purgation. They saw that He was alive and that He was present among them. However, this was a new Presence, a Presence that did not give a feeling of complete security or stability. It was connected with the newly risen humanity of Christ. This humanity was different from the former one; it was glorious and could no longer be confined to earth. His risen body could pass through closed doors, so sometimes the apostles doubted whether it was really their Master that they were seeing.

The trial of the apostles, their night of purgation, was not yet complete. The ten days between the Ascension and Pentecost brought with them trials of faith and further denudation. Then their main support, the humanity of Jesus, was definitely taken away from them.[57] Then they had nothing to rely on. **The young Church being born in the upper room and devoting herself with one accord to prayer was stripped of everything.**

The second night of purgation, the night of the spirit, is the most difficult one. The theology of spiritual life states that it is then that one encounters Mary who, through her presence, illuminates this night. And after the Ascension, this is what happened to the apostles in the upper room. They were not alone there. Mary, who never succumbed to despair and whose faith never faltered, was with them. She was among them as an example of faith and perseverance in prayer, an example of looking for the Holy Spirit to come. The apostles being truly poor – owning nothing, unable to see the humanity of Jesus – waited together with Mary. This was when the Holy Spirit, the "Father of the poor," as it is stated in the liturgy, came down upon the apostles who had been stripped of everything and left in complete emptiness. Then the strength of the Holy Spirit descended upon them. Only when they had been strengthened in this way were they sent to conquer the world for Christ.

---

[57] Réginald Garrigou-Lagrange, *The Three Ages of the Interior Life: Prelude of Eternal Life*, vol. 2, trans. M. Timthea Doyle (St. Louis, MO: B. Herder Book, 1948), 368.

TO LOVE THE CHURCH

Through Confirmation you are even more closely bonded to the Church. By receiving this sacrament, you enter into a very close spiritual bond with the bishop who performs this rite. The bishop, as a minister of the sacrament of Confirmation, partakes in the supernatural motherhood of the Church. By becoming a special channel of the graces and gifts of the Holy Spirit, the bishop "gives birth" to the fullness of Christian life in you. The liturgical texts talk about a spiritual stigma that is imprinted on the soul of the confirmed person, expressing a close and perfect bond with Christ and with the Church. When entering into a spiritual bond with the bishop, a confirmed person is called to love the Church. You should love the Church as much as Christ who "handed himself over for her" (Eph 5:25). This means loving her to the point of giving one's life for the beloved Church.

The Church is our Mother. Because of widespread secularization, our perception is that the Church is far from being supernatural. In the Apostles' Creed we profess: "I believe in . . . the holy catholic Church." This profession corresponds to an attitude expressed like this: *I devote myself trustfully to the Church as if I were to devote myself to the Person of Christ.* By your entrusting yourself to the Church, you entrust yourself to Christ. By abandoning yourself to the Church, you abandon yourself to Christ because the Church is His Mystical Body.

Henri Daniel-Rops, in his book titled *Nocturnes*, writes about a mosaic from the fourth century AD in the Bardo Museum in Tunis:

No Christian can look at that mosaic without being emotionally moved. It imperfectly portrays the front steps and colonnade of a basilica. It is made of antique stones resembling graffiti. Above the colonnade there is an inscription that causes this mosaic to become an expressive symbol. The inscription includes two significant words: *Ecclesia Mater* (Mother Church).

The fourth century was a time of great wars, of paganism that returned time and time again, and of persecution by Julian the Apostate. It was not easy or safe to openly admit that one belonged to Christ. Throughout the empire there was increasing unrest, political anarchy, and religious turmoil. Among continual threats and danger, when the blood of martyrs was still fresh in amphitheatres, someone wrote two striking and consoling words, surely engraved in the atmosphere of comforting prayer: Mother Church.

Does it require much imagination to understand those words in the same way our distant brother in Christ understood them when he arranged them with small stones into damp cement? The world that surrounded him was uncertain, and the fate of the world remained shrouded in darkness. And yet there existed a place where even danger made sense and a great hope dominated everything. It was a place where human brotherhood overcame class and race divisions, where love was stronger than death. The basilica columns and walls were only a symbol of this privileged place. An apostle said that it would be the house of the Living God forever. This place is the Church, our Mother, *Ecclesia Mater*. Many centuries and epochs have passed, and the Church still remains the same for us as she was for the faithful in that heroic century – she remains our Mother.

If the Church is the Mother, then a Christian may call himself a son of the Church. However, the word son expresses a relationship that is more than membership in human associations and parties, and other than that found in various philosophies and philosophical systems. Is the name Father (*papa*: pope), that we give to the person whom we consider to symbolize and personify the Church, not an echo of this very bond and complete trust that the African inscription, Mother Church, conveys? The role of the Church becomes particularly visible during times of threat and unrest. It has been said that the Church is dying and that along with the remnants of the past, she can be relegated to the junk heap. However, she still stands in her place like a city set on a hill visible to all. When we call for help in times of threat, our Mother the Church is invariably there. Being boundlessly patient and merciful, she always welcomes the prodigal son with joy, opening her arms to every lost sheep.

The Church believes that no betrayal is so great that it cannot be forgiven. Therefore the Church looks with indescribable compassion upon those who have rejected her for years, and softly whispers: *Does it really matter that you have wandered so far away from me? I have always been near you.*

The Church today, from the very depths of her maternal heart, offers the same support to the people of this century as she did to the people of the fourth century. In the face of great historical storms, in a world tormented so often by barbarianism, where people have lost understanding of the sense of human life, in a world that doubts everything including itself, the Church alone gives the impression that she knows well what she is aiming for. The Church alone reveals unchanging truths despite attempts to accuse her of striving for significance in public or political life. In a world possessed by violence in which man seems to be fascinated with the tragic fatality of his own death wish and the prospect of total destruction, the Church repeats a simple and much needed lesson of love. She herself received this lesson on the hillsides of Galilee, and the blood of God sealed its truth on Calvary. In repeating this lesson of love, the Church remains *Ecclesia Mater*. (Translated by author: Henri Daniel-Rops, *Nocturnes*, [Paris:Grasset, 1956])

Through Confirmation, you are very closely bonded to the Church. Being enriched by the graces of Confirmation, have you come to love her as Christ loved her? Are you interested in her life – do you call her *my Church*? Your desire to be united with Jesus will cause you to feel even more that you are a son of the Church. Seeking Jesus, you will find Him fully in His Mystical Body; by loving Him, you will begin to love the Church, which He loved to the very end, to the point of giving up His life.

APOSTOLIC RESPONSIBILITY

Love of Christ that deepens through faith begets the desire to be a witness of Christ. **Your call to sanctity and your love for the Church are also closely connected with the call to apostleship.** Reminding Christians of their obligation to witness for Christ, John Paul II said, "Only profound love for the Church can support the fervor in giving witness. Faithfulness to Christ cannot be separated from faithfulness to the Church."
The Second Vatican Council stresses that:

> Incorporated into Christ's Mystical Body through Baptism and strengthened by the power of the Holy Spirit through Confirmation, [Christians] are assigned to the apostolate by the Lord Himself...One engages in the apostolate through the faith, hope, and charity which the Holy Spirit diffuses in the hearts of all members of the Church. Indeed, by the precept of charity, which is the Lord's greatest commandment, all the faithful are impelled to promote the glory of God through the coming of His kingdom and to obtain eternal life for all men. (Second Vatican Council,

Apostolicam Actuositatem (Decree on the Apostolate of the Laity), no. 3 [Proclaimed by Pope Paul VI on november 18, 1965])

Therefore everything that you do should serve to build and expand the kingdom of God.

You have received a treasure and an extraordinary gift that you cannot keep just for yourself. This would be burying the treasure. You are to pass on this priceless treasure and share it with others. You should witness about what has been bestowed on you, what you have found, about what you love, and what the Holy Spirit has brought about in you. The more you surrender to the Holy Spirit, the more He will be able to form the image of Christ in you. The Holy Spirit, having deepened the love for the Church in your heart, will cause you to be faithful to your call to the apostolate. John Paul II once asked France, "Are you faithful to the grace of your Baptism?" This question is also directed to you: Are you faithful to the grace of holy Baptism? Are you faithful to the graces of Confirmation? Are you growing in your sense of responsibility for the image and life of your Church, diocese, and parish?

The rite of Confirmation refers to concrete forms of witnessing about Christ, which should always flow from faith and love. You are to give witness to the One who died for you and was resurrected. He also died and was resurrected for those to whom you give witness about Him. Your apostleship should be an attitude of service to others strengthened by the Holy Spirit. You should also pray to the Holy Spirit for the grace of fortitude, which is so necessary to defend faith and to undertake the difficulties of apostleship.

Confirmation will remain a sacrament unknown to you if you do not come to know the Holy Spirit. It will be a sacrament unknown to you if you do not realize that He continuously purifies and renews you. He is forming in you a filial attitude to God the Father and praying in you, in the words of a child, "Abba, Father!" If you realize this, then He will bestow on you the peace of Christ, not peace as the world gives (cf. Jn 14:27). Above all, He will draw your heart to the poor so that you will strive to help them, not only materially, but also spiritually, by proclaiming the Good News of salvation and love of God, which you will experience forevermore.

During his first pilgrimage to his homeland, on the eve of the Feast of Pentecost, John Paul II called out:

> Let Your Spirit descend!
> Let Your Spirit descend!
> And renew the face of the earth.
> This earth!

You will not see the Holy Spirit with your physical eyes, but He exists. Only through faith can you see and accept His redeeming actions. If you do not have faith, if you do not try to listen to Him, or if you actually drown out or stifle His usually quiet voice, then you "grieve the Holy Spirit of God" (Eph 4:30). An attitude such as this, if adopted by you, would be the source of His torment, the source of His abasement through His contact with you. He, who is the Spirit of Jesus sent to you, the Love of the Father and Son, continually reminds you of the words of Jesus, speaking sometimes with the force of a windstorm, but most often with the gentleness of a tiny whispering breeze. It is so easy to drown out His voice and, through your own fault, waste this extraordinary gift that is bestowed upon you in the sacrament of Confirmation.

Faith, which is a necessary condition for the work of the Holy Spirit in the soul of the confirmed, is an authentic encounter of two persons. The Holy Spirit desires to continuously deepen this encounter and, through this, to lead the soul to greater unity with Christ and to contemplation and sanctity in the service of the **beloved** Church.

CHAPTER TWELVE

THE EUCHARIST

A close interdependence exists between our faith and the sacraments. In the Constitution on the Sacred Liturgy, the Second Vatican Council emphasizes that the sacraments not only presuppose the presence of faith in those who receive them, but they also nourish faith, strengthen it, and express it.[58] Faith is always the preliminary condition for the efficacy of the sacraments, because the strength of sacraments correlates with the strength of faith. Dogmatic theology states that although the sacraments impart grace by themselves, *ex opere operato*, they remain fruitless if faith is lacking. Because of little faith, many Christians do not involve themselves in the redeeming work of Christ's death and Resurrection, which can be brought to full realization through the sacraments. Those Christians, in spite of frequent reception of the sacraments, do not develop spiritually.

---

[58] Second Vatican Council, *Sacrosanctum Concilium* (Constitution on the Sacred Liturgy), no. 59 [Proclaimed by Pope Paul VI on December 4, 1963].

LOOKING FOR THE REDEEMING ACTION OF CHRIST TO COME IN THE EUCHARIST

Perhaps you are wondering why the Eucharist and the sacrament of Penance are not transforming you, why they do not seem to bring visible results. You are not transformed because grace needs your openness and internal disposition. Look how the Church, in her wisdom, endeavors to prepare for the special graces of Christmas throughout the liturgical year. She dedicates entire weeks in Advent praying incessantly for the coming of Jesus, for His coming down to earth. She entreats in her liturgical prayers: "Let justice descend, O heavens, like dew from above" (Is 45:8). The Church desires that hunger for Jesus and for His coming continue to grow within us. The graces of Christmas dwell in our hearts to the extent of our hunger and desire for His coming. His rebirth will come within our hearts at Christmas to the extent of our preparation and our openness, therefore, to the extent of our faith. If there is no Advent, then Christmas is not adequately experienced. If you do not experience the message of Advent and, therefore, do not look for Jesus to come, then do not be surprised that Christmas seems to slip by without leaving a mark on your soul.

Just as we look for the coming of Jesus during Advent, we should also look for the coming of Jesus in the Eucharist. Jesus continually descends onto the altar, is born for us; and His birth on the altar should also be preceded by an "advent," a Eucharistic advent. A Eucharistic advent is above all an attitude of faith. It is faith in the love of Jesus who awaits you as a loved one. It is so important for you to believe that Jesus desires to come into your heart, that He desires the celebration of the Eucharist. He waits for you to receive Holy Communion because He wants to give Himself to you fully through the Most Blessed Sacrament, the main source of graces.

One of the most fundamental psychological needs in a person is the need for acceptance and love. However, do not look for acceptance and love in people through whom you will often experience disappointment and embitterment. Faith tells you that in reality you need only one acceptance, acceptance from Christ who always accepts you. John Paul II said that in Holy Communion you do not receive Him as much as He receives you; He accepts you as you are. He receives you, which means He accepts and loves you.

About 178 AD, the pagan syncretic philosopher Celsus wrote a dissertation full of hatred and sarcasm in which he mocked the Holy Mass and derided Christian dogma regarding the Incarnation and Redemption. According to Celsus, the Christian faith is sheer madness because Christians believe that their God became one among them and that they can be united with Him through a sacred banquet. This, in his opinion, is simply madness. This opinion of Celsus should be reversed. It is God's love for man that is the folly and not the Christian's belief that Christ offers Himself in the form of bread. The Eucharist is an expression of Christ's folly. His folly is His love for man and His love for you, which is beyond human prudence and foresight. You should prepare yourself for the coming of Christ in the Eucharist by believing in the folly of His love. St. Francis de Sales strove to prepare himself for the coming of Christ in the Eucharist all day so that, if asked what he was doing, he could answer that he was preparing for the Eucharistic Sacrifice.

It is so important that your faith in His love increase and that you believe ever more firmly in His ardent desire to come to you in the Eucharist. When you finally come to believe how greatly He loves you and awaits you, then you will realize that, if you delay, **in His folly of love for you, God experiences what psychology calls the torment of looking for someone to come.** When you start to believe that Jesus loves you, that in fact He waits for you, then as a consequence of your faith, the hunger for God, the desire for the Eucharist, should awaken within you a painful yearning for His coming. The torment of looking for a loved one to come is similar to the torment of love that is rejected. The more a mother loves a child who does not return, the greater is her torment in longing to see him again; how much more so if this love is the infinite love of God that you cannot even imagine. How great, then, must His torment be in looking for you to come.

Belief in His desire to meet with you will prevent you from falling into routine behavior, which is one of the greatest threats to your faith. When you come to believe fully in the infinite love of Jesus and when you realize His torment of looking for you to come to the Eucharistic Table, **then you will no longer be able to live without the Eucharist.** The hunger for God and the burning desire to meet the Lord will be within you, and routine cannot coexist with that hunger.

THE EUCHARIST AS THE CULMINATION OF FAITH

The sacrifice of Christ, according to St. Thomas Aquinas, is fruitful only in those who are united in faith and love with the passion of Christ. The greater your faith and love, the more effective the Eucharist will become in your life. Faith is sharing in the life of God and becomes actualized in a special way through the sacraments, all of which are sacraments of faith. **Through the Eucharist, you participate with the community of believers as they celebrate Christ's death and Resurrection;** you become jointly immersed in this unfathomable mystery.

> The liturgy unites us all in the explicit celebration of our faith, especially during the Eucharist. At no other time is the faith of the Church so complete. At no other time is the Church so much aware of her union with Christ who died and was resurrected, and aware that the she looks for Him to come again. At no other time do we share in the faith of our community, as at that moment when we pray together, when we make our offering together and together we unite with God's love which is in Jesus Christ. (Joseph Colomb, Le devenir de la foi, in coll. Croire et comprendre [Paris: Le Centurion, 1974], chap. 4.)

In the Eucharist Jesus immerses us in the mystery of His death, and then our conversion and transformation is being brought about; then the death of our "old" selves occurs. A resurrection and rebirth will also occur within us through the strength of sacramental action and the redeeming passion of Jesus. Our immersion in the death and Resurrection of Jesus causes new selves, conforming to the image of Jesus Himself, to begin to be born in us.

Since the Eucharist is adherence to the person of Christ, then accepting Christ and clinging to Him is fully expressed only when we partake in the Eucharist, which is the culmination of faith. During the Eucharist, Christ becomes the gift offered to the Father for our sake. Through the common royal priesthood, we also are called to give a complete offering of ourselves to God in union with Christ who offers Himself to the Father. Our adherence to Him means communion with His gift. It means giving our lives to God in order for them to be transformed and become a service to the Church and to our brothers. The purpose of the Eucharist is your conversion, your turning away from your own will so that it may gradually disappear in your service to others. You go to Holy Communion to be converted, to establish the reign of Christ in your heart from then on, and for His will to become your supreme value. **Every reception of the Eucharist should confirm your adherence to His will.** Consequently, you should wish that Jesus would foil your plans. The Eucharist should prepare you for this; it should contribute to the gradual demise of your egoism, allowing Christ to grow within you.

Since faith is reliance on Christ and the entrusting of yourself to Him, then in the Eucharist you should entrust to Him all of your affairs, fears, and anxieties. The Eucharist will then bring you peace born of faith in the redeeming power of Jesus' sacrifice. This faith means believing that He redeemed you from fear, uncertainty, and stress, and from all that destroys your spiritual life as well as your physical or mental health. Through faith you will be able to receive the fruits of Redemption.

Faith is the acknowledgement of your own helplessness and sinfulness and the awaiting of everything from God. Therefore, the Eucharist, as a *par excellence* sacrament of faith, **calls you to have the attitude of a helpless child and sinner** who longs for nothing more than being healed of his own evil. During Mass, make every effort to stand before Jesus like the leper in the Gospel and pray that Jesus will cleanse you from the leprosy of egoism, from the leprosy of your pride, the leprosy of your concern for yourself, of your hurriedness, unrest, and sadness. Then ask Him to take away your leprosy of being excessively concerned about temporal goods because all these things make the growth of Christ within you impossible.

During Mass, faith will enable you to come to know yourself, your sinfulness, and your need of Redemption. You will begin to see yourself in truth more fully to the extent of your deepening faith. You will perceive the leprosy of your sin, and then you will come to know how unworthy you are of the Eucharist and, simultaneously, how very much you need its saving action in your life.

Your growth in faith will enable you to discover **the real presence of Jesus and to discover the making present of His redemptive sacrifice.** You will begin to know Him even better, who He is, and what happens on the altar. Try to participate in the Mass as if it were for the first or for the last time in your life so that receiving the Eucharist every day does not become a routine for you that destroys your faith.

Reflect on how intensely a priest must experience his first Mass after ordination. Certainly, when he takes the Body of Christ into his hands for the first time, he becomes aware of the real presence of Somebody. His hands might even tremble at that moment, since he has faith untarnished by routine. Imagine the First Holy Communion of a convert who, after preparing for and receiving the sacrament of Baptism, receives the Eucharist. He may receive the Body of Christ with trembling lips, since his faith is so strong and alive that present on his lips is God Himself, and that it is God Himself who enters his heart. He may believe that he finds himself before the face of a tremendous unfathomable mystery, full of majesty – *misterium tremendum.*

KENOSIS OF CHRIST

Faith allows you to see that **your hands and lips that receive Jesus are always unclean** – even when you are in a state of sanctifying grace – because you are always a sinner, and the hands and lips of a sinner always remain unworthy and, therefore, unclean. "How very unworthy I feel I am, of this grace of the altar, which I used to approach so boldly," Cardinal S. Wyszynski wrote in his prison notes of 7 April 1955.[59] Just think, you receive Jesus with your lips that can kill with words. Your words sometimes wound and are the source of harm and unhappiness, instead of uttering blessings. And yet, these sinful lips come into contact with the highest sanctity of God. If you consider all of this, you will come to know the mystery that theology calls *kenosis* (Greek: a complete humiliation).

---

[59] Stefan Cardinal Wyszynski, *Zapiski Wiezienne*, 4th ed. (Warsaw: Soli Deo, 1995).–Ed.

The Eucharist is a kenosis – the Self-humiliation of true God and true Man, since Jesus in His utmost sanctity comes into contact with your sinfulness and your unworthiness. This does not mean, however, that you should avoid the Eucharist, for when you receive the Eucharist, He makes you more worthy of receiving Him again. Jesus waits for you with His love. He wants to come in order to transform you, to sanctify you, and to make you increasingly more worthy of His coming.

St. John the Apostle said, "If we say, 'We are without sin,' we deceive ourselves, and the truth is not in us" (1 Jn 1:8). We are all sinners, and we are all unworthy to receive Jesus. Think of your lips as unclean, but you should also await the Eucharist to remove that uncleanliness – that leprosy of sin, that leprosy of egoism – from your lips and from your heart and soul. Jesus desires this so much that He wants it to be done even at the price of His great humiliation, at the price of His kenosis. It is in the light of faith that you will see how the Eucharist is the great Self-humiliation of Christ. He strips Himself of His divine dignity and humiliates Himself by the very fact that His majesty and His humanity are hidden in the material form of bread and wine. He strips Himself from His due praise and honor. When you come to Him with your sinful hands, with sinful lips, and a sinful heart, this is a further kenosis for Him.

St. Louis Marie Grignon de Montfort advises us to invite Mary to participate in the Eucharist with us. **The presence of the Immaculate Mary close to us,** especially during the Eucharist, **is a great mystery for us, and it is a solution to the problem of the kenosis of Christ.** Those who find it difficult to acknowledge the need and importance of the Marian way to Christ are convinced that Mary cannot stand between themselves and Christ, for she would overshadow Jesus. However, in the light of faith, in the light of the knowledge of God's holiness, in the knowledge of your own great unworthiness and sinfulness, you will find that this situation is not the case. When you ask Mary to stand between you and Christ, you become closer to Him because **when you ask her to stand between you and Christ, you do it so that she may spare Him kenosis,** His Self-humiliation. Only her hands are clean and were never unclean; they were and always will be immaculate. Here are the only human hands and the only human lips that are clean and immaculate, that are worthy to touch the Body of Christ. When you strive to lessen the Self-humiliation of Christ by asking Mary to receive Him for you and through you, then you give praise to the kenosis of the True God and True Man. You link the attitude of humility, an attitude of acknowledgement that you are a sinner, with faith in His incredible love for you. This love, at the price of the Self-humiliation that is beyond your imagination, wants to bestow upon you the fruits of the Redemption.

CHAPTER THIRTEEN

LISTENING INTENTLY TO THE WORD OF GOD

A close interdependence exists between faith and the Word of God as well as between faith and the sacraments. Reading the Holy Bible requires faith as well as active cooperation and conversion. The actualization of the Word of God is required in everyday life, which should be a life flowing from faith. Faith is the response to the Word of God; it is listening intently to the Word in order to live it every day.

ENCOUNTERING THE WORD OF GOD

We can regard biblical text in two ways: **impersonally, as an object** – when it is seen as something that we examine or as an aid in finding the solution to a problem that interests us – or **personally, as a subject,** when the text we read becomes for us a "mystery" as explained by Gabriel Marcel.[60] If you read the Holy Scriptures with the intention of broadening your religious knowledge, it means that you regard them as an object. The Bible treated as an object is simply a "thing." This relationship with the Holy Scriptures is necessary; however, it is insufficient.

Certainly for the Church, the Word of God is the principle source from which we gain knowledge of God; thus it should sometimes be regarded as an object. Nevertheless, the Holy Scriptures are also inspired text and a source of revelation; therefore, **our relationship with the revealed text should primarily be a personal one.** In fact, the Bible is not a "thing" but, above all, it is "Somebody." Christ is most fully present with us in the Eucharist but, in another way, He is also present and alive in the Bible. When reading the Holy Scriptures, you encounter the living and true Christ through the gift of **faith**, which He Himself gives to you. The Church states that the Eucharistic table has a double meaning. It is the table of the Word of God where the faithful receive, through **faith**, the revealed Word of God. It is also the table of the Body of the Lord where the faithful are nourished with the Body and Blood of the Lord when celebrating the "sacrament of faith." Therefore, it is right to say that one should approach the Bible in the same way as one would approach the table of the Lord. That is why, when you take the Bible into your hands, you should do this with respect, veneration, and profound faith. This should be done with a different gesture than reaching for any other religious book since this is a book filled with God's presence.

---

[60] "Christian existentialist philosopher (1889-1973)." *The New Catholic Encyclopedia*, 2nd.ed., s.v. "Marcel, Gabriel."—Ed.

THE PRESENCE OF GOD IN THE WORD

Every person affects the environment by his presence; this does not occur with things. Only when we meet a person do we encounter their presence and, through this, enter into either a desirable or inconvenient sphere of their influence. The Holy Bible is "Someone;" it is the presence of God. Therefore, when taking it into your hands, you enter into the realm of that very Presence. It becomes a "mystery" for you, a truth that grasps you and into which you are immersed.

You will find your Lord in the Bible, and that is why your contact with the revealed text has a special meaning. **It is contact with God who loves you and desires to affect you with His grace.** This contact leads you to inner conversion – its greatest purpose. You should, therefore, not read the Bible just to satisfy your curiosity, or to gain knowledge, or to find a solution to a problem that is nagging you – although this will be needed at times. You should take advantage of this form of contact with the Lord in the hope that He will bestow the grace of conversion on you. **If you enter into a person-to-person relationship with Christ, who is present throughout the inspired text, this text will permeate you.** Then you will begin to **listen intently to the Word of God,** understand better the thoughts and desires of Jesus, and begin to know Him even better. St. Jerome warns: "Ignorance of the Holy Scriptures is ignorance of Christ." Listening intently to the Word of God will influence your choices and decisions. You will want them to be in accordance with His teachings and His desires. **Reading of the Holy Scriptures is fundamental to your growth in faith and of your sharing in God's life.** It is looking at oneself and surrounding realities as though through the eyes of God. God reveals Himself to us through the intercession of the Word, leading us toward love through knowledge of Himself. He reveals Himself so that, by believing in His Word, we may adhere to Him and entrust ourselves to Him. If you attempt to share in the thoughts and desires of Jesus in faith, then they will eventually become your thoughts and desires. If you remain in the realm of His presence, the genuine Presence, then you will become like Him in the same way that you become like the people you associate with: "like father, like son." By listening to the Word of God and taking in its essence, you will begin to empathize with Christ in His experiences in the Gospel and in what He was presently experiencing. **Your intense contact with Christ who is present in the Word of God will cause you to identify with Him even more.**

Every word recorded in the New Testament and every gesture of Jesus is an expression of this mystery of the Presence. You should allow it to overwhelm you; you should learn to listen intently to it. This unimaginable Presence requires your particular openness that will, in time, cause your total transfiguration – so that **you become as if transformed into Christ.** The purpose of your life will then be achieved – Christ increasing within you and reaching His fullness.

THE ROLE OF THE WORD OF GOD IN PRAYER

The presence of Christ in the Word of God will overwhelm your interior life and your prayer. Listening intently to the Word of God will cause you to meditate on the words, which will be engraved deeply into your heart. They will later come to mind during moments of prayer that will then become prayer based on the Bible; and they will also come to mind in moments of making decisions. Have you already asked yourself, *What is the role of the Bible in my prayer?*

Christ often used a specific literary form, the parable, which is an expanded symbol that draws your attention and engages you. Because of this, when you read the parable of the Good Shepherd for example, you can truly recognize yourself among the sheep led by the shepherd. You can also imagine yourself as the lost sheep loved by Christ the Good Shepherd, who never stops searching for you and, when He finds you, sets you on His shoulders with great joy. The symbolism of the parables of Christ draws you into the realm of His works. **In such a simple and accessible way, He teaches you to love and to believe in love.** If it happens that you have had a great fall and your soul is shrouded in darkness, then maybe you will recall the parable of the Prodigal Son, which will let you believe once again that He has never stopped loving you. The parable will teach you the attitude of the repentant son who, with amazement and gratefulness, welcomes the joy of the forgiving father. Similarly, when some storms occur in your life you may be reminded of the storm on the Sea of Galilee. Then you will realize that, just as Jesus slept in the storm-tossed boat of the apostles, He also "sleeps" now in the boat of your heart. Nevertheless, He is present within you, and when He is there, nothing bad can happen to you. All this may help you to include the Word of God in your prayer, which will allow you to regain an inner peace.

Through your reading of the Bible, a true image of God will be formed in you. You will avoid distorting His image, which so often happens. Maybe you are afraid of Him, or maybe you do not believe enough in His love because your love is so little. Your love should continue to grow until you die. **Prayerful meditation on the Bible will teach you about the love of God, who loves you incessantly, because He is Love.**

Meeting with Christ who is present in the Word of God will also help you to discover God in the world around you. It will teach you to interpret the many symbols through which you can discover His presence in nature and even in the phenomena of civilization and culture. Sheep, for example, reminded St. John Vianney of the love of the Good Shepherd. The sight of sheep deepened the awareness in him of the great love Jesus had for him as a shepherd of a parish. Moreover, it reminded him of Jesus the Good Shepherd's love for those whom He had entrusted into St. John's love and care in order for the saint to be their shepherd. The sound of a mountain stream reminded St. John Vianney of the words in the Gospel about the "living water" welling up to eternal life (cf. Jn 4:14; 7:37-39). Someone once said of himself that he enjoyed watching the lights on the streets and in houses, and the lights of passing cars at night. It reminded him vividly of fragments in the Bible, especially the fragments in the Gospel according to St. John stating that Jesus is the light of the world. Every light, therefore, became a symbol of Christ for him, bringing to mind "the true light, which enlightens everyone" (Jn 1:9).

If you also want your prayer to be based on the Bible, you have to be like Mary from Bethany. In Bethany, with His friends Mary, Martha, and Lazarus, Jesus found a place of shelter and rest for Himself. When the final days of His life were approaching, knowing that the Pharisees were spying on Him, He went into hiding in Bethany. Earlier, though, when Jesus came to their home, Mary sat at His feet and listened intently to every word spoken by Him; she behaved as if she were before a tabernacle. When a busy Martha asked Jesus to speak to her sister Mary about letting her do all the serving, He answered her, "Mary has chosen the better part and it will not be taken from her" (Lk 10:42). **This "better part" is to be beside Christ, to sit at His feet and listen intently, with faith, to His words spoken to us through the Bible.**

Mary, listening to and contemplating Jesus, the Word Incarnate, must have been His great joy. Whereas, we, so often busy and anxious about many things, feel that we do not have the time to read the Bible. For Mary, however, there was nothing more important than the fact that He, the Master, was there in her home. The most appropriate place she found for herself was at His feet.

According to the thought of Jean Guitton, the Blessed Virgin Mary could be called the Virgin of Meditation [*Virgo Meditans*].[61] Mary's hymn, the *Magnificat*, is a testimony of how much the Bible was a source of life for her. It is a testimony of prayer based on the Word of the Lord. The Bible was her "nourishment" and source of prayer.

For thirty years, Mary absorbed the divine presence of her Son. **That is why her face portrayed the face of Jesus in**

---

[61] Jean Guitton, *La Vierge Marie*, Edition: Nouvelle éd. revue et augmentée (Paris: Aubier, 1954); Jean Marie Pierre Guitton, *The Virgin Mary*, trans. A. Gordon Smith (New York : Kenedy, 1952).–Ed.

the most perfect way, and this is the source of her greatness. How important it must have been to Christ to create this Masterpiece, **His most perfect image,** since He devoted Himself to Mary for as many as thirty years. She continuously absorbed His thoughts, His desires, and His will, thus becoming more and more united with her Son.

You encounter the presence of Jesus in the pages of the Bible. You should, therefore, just as Mary did, absorb His thoughts and desires in order to later live by them. You should imitate Mary completely, to the end, in becoming open to the great work of Christ who transforms us into His image.

The Bible should be a place for you to encounter Christ who has loved you to the end. He desires to form His image in you also, just as He did in His beloved Mother.

PRAYER AS AN ACTUALIZATION OF FAITH

P rayer and faith are not separate realities that are merely mutually dependent or exist side by side. Prayer is always closely connected with the reality of faith; it is the meeting of a person with God in faith, and ultimately, it is a form of the actualization of faith. If faith is adhering to Christ and entrusting oneself to Him, then prayer is the giving of oneself in complete devotion to Christ, to be accepted and transformed by Him in a new way. If faith is the acknowledgement of one's own helplessness and the awaiting of everything from God, then prayer is the existential calling of spiritual poverty and inner emptiness of a person so that the Holy Spirit may fill him with His presence and strength. As one's faith develops, prayer becomes purer and more ardent. Prayer, as an actualization of faith, is marked by the dynamism of conversion. Similarly, the Eucharist and the Word of the Lord lead a person toward transformation and toward conversion.

THE EXAMPLE OF CHRIST

When we read the words of the Gospel, we quickly discover that the Good News confuses us. The Gospel is so contrary to our natural tendencies that it seems an unceasing paradox. The Gospel overturns our human concepts. Christ Himself did just this.

He was awaited for thousands of years. Everything was oriented toward this unique event in the history of the world, which was to be the coming of the Messiah, the coming of the One who would perform the work of Redemption. After such a long period of expectation, Jesus revealed Himself only to the shepherds and the Wise Men. Then, for over thirty years, He led a secluded life far from activity, at least in the sense of the activity that was expected of a Messiah. In the eyes of the world, those years appear to be wasted; for if someone is awaited for thousands of years, he should give the most of himself. Multitudes of people were waiting, and there was Christ, "wasting" thirty years in Nazareth. When this wasted time – in terms of human activism – was over, Christ showed Himself by the river Jordan and was proclaimed by the Holy Spirit Himself. Then Jesus retreated and went into the desert. Thus we are yet again confused and cannot understand Jesus' attitude at all. We would like to take Him aside and rebuke Him as Peter the Apostle once did. We would say, *Lord, what on earth were You doing?*

Multitudes were waiting, and yet You went off to pray again. Have You not already prayed for so many years? Yet He who would later say, "The harvest is abundant but the laborers are few" (Lk 10:2), left the harvest and went into the desert to pray incessantly for forty days. Does this not amaze us?

The Evangelist Mark writes, "Rising very early before dawn, he left and went off to a deserted place, where he prayed" (Mk 1:35). Pay attention to this detail, "before dawn"; this means that it was still night. **Christ, wanting to pray, deprived Himself of His sleep.** Astonished, we would again want to cry out, *Lord, did you really need this prayer at night at the cost of your health?* Each day of Christ's apostleship was exhausting. Even in the evening people would come from the whole city or surrounding area and bring all who were ill and possessed to Him. It is difficult to say when His daily work ended. It may have ended at midnight, for the multitudes left Him unwillingly. After such a hard day and an exhausting evening, Jesus still deprived Himself of His little sleep.

When we speak of Jesus being besieged continually by the multitudes, we have to say that this was closely related to His praying in solitude. There is an especially important message for you hidden in this: in order for your contact with people to be fruitful, **you have to know beforehand how to leave for seclusion.** You have to appreciate a time of desert in your life. How great a role the time of the desert must have played in the lives of the saints. Think about how much John the Baptist needed solitude in the desert, and how decisive was St. Ignatius Loyola's life as a hermit in Manresa, or the role of the hermitage in the life of St. Benedict in Subiaco.

Contemporary man, affected by activism, seems to think that he must continuously give more of himself, **but what really is to be given?** One might think that Christ, who was so completely united with the Father, did not need to pray at all. But He continued to do so regardless of His need to sleep. And it was always like this. Being besieged by people was always the result of having withdrawn to **meet with God.** However, if on your part there is no withdrawal to pray and meditate, but only an escape from people into your own personal affairs, then another kind of siege will occur, a siege of your own egoism. This will also be a desert for you, but not a life-giving one as was Christ's desert or the deserts of the saints; it will be a desert of destruction and not of life.[62]

THE PRIORITY OF PRAYER

Some fundamental questions arise here: How much time do you devote to prayer in your everyday life? What place does prayer have on your list of the most important things you are to do? Before what and after what do you place it? **Does it head the list** of your life's affairs, or is it the least important? What about your day of recollection? What about your examination of conscience, which is looking at yourself before the face of God? The answers to these questions will indicate **what is more important than God in your life.**

At this point you may begin by objecting that with a whole mass of duties it is difficult for you to find the time to pray. During a meeting with priests, Cardinal Lercaro, the Archbishop of Bologna, spoke with his unique fervor and

---

[62] Alessandro Pronzato, *Ho voglia di pregare* (Torino, Italy: Gribaudi, 1971), 64.

ardor about the necessity of half an hour of meditation every day. During the discussion after the conference meeting, one of the young priests stood up and said:

"Of course, your Eminence, in theory this is clear and simple; one should meditate...but when? My day looks like this: I get up in the morning at 6:30; at 7:00 I say Mass; after that I listen to confessions, then religious instruction, and lunch; after lunch I have lessons with the boys in the oratory; then I visit the sick, I work in the parish office, and I have pastoral meetings. In the evening I work with youth groups until about midnight. Where am I to find time for half an hour of meditation if I can barely find time to say the breviary?" "You're right," said the Cardinal, "you really don't have time for half an hour of meditation. Your activities 'smother' you to such an extent that you have no time to pray. If you cannot afford half an hour to meditate, you should meditate not for half an hour, but for one and a half hours." (A. Pronzato, *Ho voglia di pregare*, 113.)

Of course, this was not intended to be a bright, paradoxical response. The tragedy of our Christian activism is that **activities really do smother us.** This young, zealous priest who was devoting himself to God and to saving souls, was so smothered by activism that he needed a greater antidote.

If you look at yourself in the light of faith, you will understand that **the more suppressed you are with activities, the more time you should dedicate to prayer.** Otherwise you will be empty; you will have the impression that you are giving something, but this will only be an illusion. **You cannot give what you do not have.** It could be said to the young priest who was talking with Cardinal Lercaro, *What of it, that you devote so much time to your ministerial work, that you spend so much time with the boys in the oratory, that you visit the sick, that you hear confessions, and have pastoral meetings? All of this is like trying to carry water in a sieve.*

The exhausted, overworked, busy priest trying to carry water in a sieve does not realize who is the One who really makes all the decisions. To say that this priest has no faith would be too emphatic, but his faith is undoubtedly poor. With his attitude he seems to say, *It is I who am making history, be it only in my own area in the parish or some other place; it is I who decides who will be a believer; the salvation of others depends solely on my work.*

Meanwhile, **everything depends on God**; it is He who decides, and only He can give you strength. If He involves you in His work it does not mean that you are irreplaceable. So many times God has shown us that He can manage very well without us. If you have seen this in your life then you have received a great grace. God needs us only because He Himself has wanted it. He can save people who have not attended classes in religious education, as we have often witnessed. There are some people who come to church and to confession and have never attended a single religion lesson, and yet the seed sown by God has formed new shoots in their souls. **God** does not need human intervention but, despite this, **He wants to involve us in His redeeming works of saving the world.** If, however, we feel that everything depends on us and on our work, then we are trying to carry water in a sieve.

When overworked, it is easy to forget that we should first of all want to have an audience with the One upon whom everything depends, who holds the fate of the world and the fate of each one of us in His hands.

In the light of faith, the most important activity in our day is prayer. It must take precedence over all other activities. **Contact with God determines the value and importance of our work.** Its efficacy depends on what is, as it were, in the back room; therefore it may depend on your knees that might be hurting very much from kneeling.

According to John Paul II, it is not important what you do; it is important who you are. It is important that you are like this pope, a person of faith and prayer. When a Christian, as a disciple of Christ, stops being a person of prayer, he becomes useless to the world; he becomes like tasteless salt worth only to be "trampled underfoot" (cf. Mt 5:13).

The issue of prayer is a major issue in our Christian vocation. By praying, we not only pay homage to Christ on our own behalf, but we worship Him in the name of the whole world, which either does not know how, is unable to, or does not want to pray. One thing is certain: if we do not pray, no one will need us. The world does not need empty souls and hearts. When we ask what the relationship is between prayer and action, then the priority of prayer and sacrifice should be emphasized more than action. We can bring God into the lives of children whom we catechize at home or in school only to the extent of our having begged for it earlier on our knees. The issue of the relationship between prayer and action can be summarized in this statement: all authentic action is born of prayer and contemplation. For everything that is great in this world comes from God; everything that is great in this world is born of sacrifice and prayer.

KINDS OF PRAYER

Prayer is the crucial issue for every Christian. **You are as much a Christian as you are capable of praying.** Prayer and its particular stages are signs and indications of your closeness to or distance from God. The stages on your path to God are indicated by various stages of prayer. At each one there is a different form and kind of prayer because prayer is the expression of your bond with God.

There may arise in your life a stage of dryness at prayer, stripped of emotions. It is then difficult to pray. Therefore, you may be tempted to give up with the thought that this prayer is pointless. However, it is then that your prayer may have special value because you will begin to undertake the effort to pray all the more on account of God alone.

A particularly meaningful story told by one of the saints is the tale of the king's musician, their mutual love, and the drama of the musician. It is a true tragedy for a musician to lose his hearing, and this is exactly what happened to this musician. He began to lose his hearing and very quickly became stone-deaf. His music stopped giving him pleasure, and he went through sheer torment when playing his instruments. Nevertheless, the king still wanted to listen to his music, so the musician continued playing, but now exclusively for the king.

You feel good when you feel the presence of God while praying. Prayer can then be something appealing, and you may be convinced that you are praying only to God. However, you will discover the fuller truth about your prayer when, like the musician who lost his hearing, you become "deaf" in your contact with God. You will then be convinced that when you were praying because of God you were also, to a certain extent, praying because of yourself – and that your prayer was not fully free from self-interest nor was it pure.

Once you start experiencing a state of dryness in prayer, do not give in to the temptation of resignation because it is then, when you feel nothing, that you are praying solely for the King.

We must continuously learn to pray. It is a task that stands before us at all times. The actual form of our prayer cannot be sufficient for us. We should continually advance and develop it. When we speak of prayer, **praying in words** most often comes to mind. In this form of prayer, we should emphasize the important value of ejaculatory prayers in which we humiliate ourselves before God, expressing our gratitude or asking for the grace of holiness. While praying in words, we must remember that we should pray for that which God expects from us. It cannot be prayer drowned in words. Jesus clearly warns us that we should not pray as pagans who "think that they will be heard because of their many words" (Mt 6:7).

Faith has a decisive influence on **what you pray for** and on the **intensity** of your prayer. If faith changes our mentality and tells us to put God in first place then, to the extent of its growth, our prayer will be increasingly simplified. It will become more and more subordinate to the work of the Holy Spirit (cf. Rom 8:26-27) and ever more concerned with matters of the Kingdom. "But seek first the kingdom [of God] and his righteousness, and all these things will be given you besides" (Mt 6:33). The word "first" is of the utmost importance here. For you, it means to put God in first place. Do not resign from your own pace of effort, but **leave all concern for yourself and for the results of your actions to the One whose will is to bestow you with boundless love.** Then in your prayer you will fulfill the call of Jesus addressed to St. Catherine of Sienna: **"You think of me, and I will think of you."**

Besides praying in words, which can take the form of a prayer of supplication, a prayer of gratitude, or a prayer of adoration, a simpler method exists for our contact with God. **God wants us to continually simplify our way of praying.** If we are to pray without ceasing according to the Bible, then our prayer must constantly be simplified because we will not be able to pray in a difficult way for very long. There will come a time in our spiritual life when it will be easier to think about God than to talk to Him. We will then move on to **simple prayers of thought focused on God**, which could be called **memory of the presence of God.** This is a simpler form of prayer than praying in words. It requires a lot less effort. You only have to think of Jesus and realize that the One who loves you is close to you. Similarly when you are preparing to receive the Eucharist, it is sufficient that you turn your will and love-filled thought toward Him in the preceding hours. Prayer of thought can be an expression of

faith, which means to strive to think with the thoughts of Jesus or Mary. This should be a thought full of serenity and joy. And the "reason for our joy" is Mary. Hence, our optimistic way of thinking, in the supernatural sense, is like sharing in the thoughts of Mary herself. The prayer of thought is a simple one, though it requires attention and care so that it may occur as frequently as possible in our lives. Therefore, try to remember and think about the fact that Jesus loves you, that He loves those whom you love, and those whom you care about. This kind of prayer of faith will bring you inner peace.

God may desire to simplify our prayer even further. He may want us to become completely silent. Just as we can pray with words or thoughts, we can also pray with silence. However, not everyone agrees with this form of prayer. Many have doubts whether or not this is a waste of time because during this time nothing is happening. However, remaining in **silence** is quite an advanced form of prayer, whether it is before the Most Blessed Sacrament or in the presence of Our Lady. Charles de Foucauld wrote that "to pray is to look at Jesus loving Him." This form of prayer may take on a form called **the prayer of simplicity** or **the prayer of simple regard.** If you have to entertain certain people with words while with them, this indicates that they are more or less strangers to you. With a person who is close to you, you can be silent, and you will not feel uncomfortable. It is this silence, so expressive in its simplicity, that is the criteria of closeness between two people. Jesus wants us to be able to calm ourselves before Him so that we simply look at Him and are close to Him, without unnecessary words.

It may happen that the prayer of silence also becomes too difficult for you. Then yet another form of prayer may arise – **the prayer of gesture. You can pray with a smile,** for example, even if this seems odd at first. God really does want our contact with Him to be very simple; He wants it to be the contact of a child with his Father, the contact of a child with his Mother. If you love someone, you can say so much to them with a smile. You can make excellent contact with that person. Why then should we not smile at God or Mary? This is the prayer of gesture. A smile is a symbolic gesture through which we express our closeness, gratitude, love, and joy to someone. It is a symbolic form containing many connotations so that a smile can mean something else each time one smiles. Thus, you do not have to exert yourself to express everything in words. God knows that you are smiling at Him, and He knows why you are doing so. Your smile toward God and your joy flowing from faith is a genuine, *par excellence* prayer.

St. Thérèse of Lisieux shows us another moving example of the symbolic prayer of gesture. About two weeks before her death, when she was gravely ill, she was given a beautiful rose from the convent courtyard. She started plucking the petals and covered her crucifix with them in great piety and love. Then, with each petal, she wiped the wounds of the nailed hands and feet of Jesus. With this symbolic gesture, as she stated, she wanted to relieve the pain of the Crucified Lord, to dry His tears.[63] Another time, relates Celine, "I found her touching with her finger-tips the nails and the crown of thorns of her Jesus. When I asked what she was doing, she answered – in a tone of mild

---

[63] "Yellow Notebook," September 14, 1897 in *Thérèse: Last Conversations*, 190.

embarrassment that I had noticed her, 'I am removing His nails and lifting the crown of thorns from His Brow!'"[64] There is no substitute for a gesture of this kind. This prayer expressed her desire to relieve the crucified Jesus of His pain. It was an expression of her particular love for the One who was the Spouse of her soul and had been crucified by sins.

St. Leopold Mandic of Padua, a great confessor of our time who spent many hours in the confessional, prayed with the **gesture of showing empty hands.** When hearing confessions, he held his hands in his lap as if, in this way, wanting to tell Jesus, *You see Lord, I am not capable of helping the one who is kneeling before me. I am able to give him nothing. Fill these hands with your grace.* If he had tried to continually repeat this to Jesus, he would have been exhausted; besides, while listening to confessions, it would not have been possible. You can also pray with this attitude of being poor in spirit in various situations. You can hold your hands in the same way, being aware that it is always a gesture of petition for Jesus to fill your empty hands with His graces and to make you an instrument of His works.

THE PRAYER OF THE POOR IN SPIRIT

A close bond exists between faith and prayer as well as between humility and prayer. Someone said, "You learn to pray best in moments when you cannot pray." This is the very opposite of what we would imagine. When it is difficult for

---

[64] Sister Genevieve of the Holy Face [Celine Martin], *A Memoir of My Sister, St. Thérèse,* trans. Carmelite Sisters of New York (New York: P.J. Kenedy & Sons, 1959), 120.

you to pray, when you are not successful in your prayers, then you receive an exceptional opportunity from God for learning how to pray. **The secret of prayer is being hungry for God.** This hunger in us for God comes from a much deeper level than feelings or speech. A person whose memory and imagination are tormented by a multitude of useless and even evil thoughts or images can sometimes, under the pressure exerted by them, pray much better in his troubled heart than the one who has untarnished thoughts and who is able to offer easy acts of love. In our hearts, these experiences give rise to **the prayer of faith of the poor in spirit.** In prayer, we should be humble and helpless. If we are unable to pray, then the Holy Spirit Himself will descend into our humble soul and will pray in us with beseeching such as cannot be expressed in words (cf. Rom 8:26).

You can experience many difficulties in prayer, but remember that these difficulties are what cause your prayer to be the prayer of the poor in spirit. You should be grateful, therefore, that you experience difficulties. These difficulties can be of various kinds; for example, they can be the result of fatigue. St. Thérèse of the Child Jesus wrote, "I should be desolate for having slept (for seven years) during my hours of prayer and my *thanksgivings*; well, I am not desolate. I remember that *little children* are as pleasing to their parents when they are asleep as well as when they are wide awake... Finally, I remember that: *'The Lord knows our weakness, that he is mindful that we are but dust and ashes.'*"[65] Therefore fatigue can become the material out of which the Lord will shape in you the prayer of a humble person, one poor in spirit. Maybe

---

[65] Thérèse, *Story of a Soul*, 165.

you will be able to take advantage of other situations that cause your prayer to become a prayer of the poor in spirit.

If prayer comes easily for you, this is also a gift from God that should not be scorned. However, it is **the struggle to get through to God that brings about the true progress of your prayer**. This struggle is an expression of hunger for God, which constitutes the essence of prayer. The progress of your prayer is brought about **through the desire to enter the realm of God, opening yourself to Him, and allowing the Holy Spirit to pray within you**. This desire itself is most essential in prayer. Are the results of your prayer then so important? It is important that you desire, that you really want to pray. The greater the hunger for God in you, the better. Through prayer, therefore, you should struggle to get through to God, and you should come to love this. God will accept all of your desires even though you feel that they are of no great value. He loves humble gifts, He does not want beautiful flowers, but prefers simple and plain ones from the meadow because they do not feed our pride. Someone once said that among all gifts God likes humble gifts the best – gifts that are not something to be proud of. It is this that is needed also in prayer. God accepts each one of your gifts, even though it may not be worth more than a handful of dust. Simply by accepting your gifts, He will make each of them priceless. Your prayer may be just like a handful of dust, but it will become priceless because God, your loving Father, accepts it. He accepts it with the same joy as a mother accepts a little flower from a small child since it is the thought that counts.

It may also be that you do not have anything to offer God in prayer. Then you will give Him your "nothingness," your complete helplessness. Offer everything to the Lord. Offer yourself to His disposal, such as you are: small, helpless, and poor in spirit. This is the best prayer, the best because it is in accordance with the first Beatitude. The prayer of the poor in spirit is a prayer of a man who is empty in the sense of an emptiness that summons the descent of the Lord – the descent of the Holy Spirit. When God sees a soul such as this, stripped of its own strength, He then descends into it with His strength. Blessed are the poor in spirit; blessed are those who pray the prayer of the poor in spirit.

THE ROSARY OF THE BLESSED VIRGIN MARY

On New Year's Day in St. Peter's Basilica in Rome on the Solemnity of Mary, Mother of God, John Paul II prayed:

> Blessed are you who believed! Blessed are you! The Evangelist speaks of you: "Mary kept all these things, reflecting on them in her heart." You are the memory of the Church. The Church learns from you, Mary, that to be a Mother means to be a living memory, that is to say, to keep and reflect on in one's heart, the joyful, glorious, as well as sorrowful matters of the faithful. Mary kept, remembered and meditated in her heart the matters of her Son and of herself as a Mother who is involved in everything relating to Him. She was the memory in the early Church and remained the memory throughout all ages in the history of the Church.

In the words of the Holy Father, Mary is the memory of the Church. In her life there were the Annunciation, the Presentation of her Son at the temple, and the finding of the twelve year old Jesus. If the Gospel states that she meditated on and kept everything in her heart, then that means that **she prayed by means of these events.** Returning continually in her memory to everything that was important in her Son's life and in her own, it was as though she prayed her rosary without moving from one bead to another. For instance, Mary could not forget that first, most important event in her life, the Annunciation. She lived the joyous events, as well as those connected with the Passion and the Resurrection of her Son. This was her prayer.

If you pray the rosary, you are praying her prayer. Then you are like an image of the Blessed Mother. **You imitate her in this way of keeping and reflecting on the mysteries of the Son and Mother.** She is the memory of the Church, the memory of those events for each of us. Each one of those events is to be alive in us. Meditating on them, you make contact with these mysteries and they become a channel of grace for you. **To love the rosary is to love the Gospel. It is to love Mary also, and to love all that she pondered on and kept in her heart and all that made up her life.**

A MAN OF INCESSANT PRAYER

Guy de Larigaudie was an exceptional man of prayer. It would seem that he was a man to whom God never refused anything. He was a great explorer of continents – the first to drive by car from France to Indochina, and he was the leader of a French youth movement. Guy de Larigaudie was someone who had come to love God with all his heart and, therefore, was also able to fully love his neighbor and the world. Beneath a photo of him there is a significant note: "Smiling Sainthood." His religious attitude was characterized primarily by a **prayer of affirmation for the world** through a faith-filled admiration of its beauty. For if one loves God, then one also loves the world. In his notes he wrote:

> Everything should be loved: an orchid that suddenly blooms in the jungle, a beautiful horse, the gesture of a child, a jest, a woman's smile. All encountered beauty should be admired; it should be uncovered, even though it is wallowing in the mud, and raised up to God. (Editor translation of Guy de Larigaudie, *Etoile au grand large* [Paris: Éditions du Seuil, 1943], 36)

Of course, this does not mean that in Guy de Larigaudie's life there were no struggles or sacrifices, no trials of faith or brave decisions, for sainthood cannot be easy.

> To feel deeply within oneself all the filth, debauchery and raging human instincts and yet, rise above all this, without sinking into it, as if one is walking on a dried swamp allowing oneself to be uplifted by a kind of lightness that does not allow one's feet to sink in. To remain in God's love as in the purity of a sunrise shining brilliantly on the vast expanse of a marsh without the body sinking into the mud. (pp. 11-12)

> She was probably Métis. She had splendid shoulders and the animal beauty of those of

mixed-blood with thick lips and huge eyes. She was beautiful, wildly beautiful. There was truly only one thing left to do. I didn't do it. I mounted my horse and rode away at full speed without looking back, crying out of desperation and rage. I trust that on Judgment Day, if I have nothing else to give, I will be able to offer God, like a bouquet, all those embraces, which, out of love for Him, I did not want to know. (p. 17)

Chastity is possible if it is built on the foundation of prayer:

It is possible, beautiful and enriching if it is supported on a positive base: a living total love of God, solely capable of satisfying the immense need for love that fills the human heart. (p. 12)

Guy de Larigaudie loved dancing, singing, and taking risks. He was an excellent swimmer and skier. He took in all the joys, but throughout all of his feelings and experiences there flowed a continuous rhythm of conversation with God, brimming over with faith.

The beautiful foreign women could not understand that even during the most captivating dance music, my heart inside was keeping the rhythm of prayer and that prayer was stronger than their charm or attractiveness. (pp. 36-37)

In his prayer for beauty he asked:

My God, grant that our sisters, these young girls, have bodily harmony, that they smile and dress with good taste. Grant that they be sound in body and mind, that they be wholesome and of transparent soul. Let them be the purity and grace of our harsh lives. Grant that they be simple and maternal toward us without being dishonest or flirting. Grant that nothing evil slips between us and that we, boys and girls, may be for one another not a source of downfall but of enrichment... From Tahiti to Hollywood, on the coral beaches or the decks of steamships – to the rhythm of the dance – I have held in my arms the most beautiful women in the world. Although fascinating to conquer, I had no intention of picking any one of these offered flowers. Yet, I myself considered worthless all the human reasons to run away. It was solely for the love of God that, my body aching, I played indifference. (p. 35)

Regarding the Eucharist, Larigaudie says:

Daily Communion each morning has been for me a bath of living water that strengthens and relaxes all the muscles, the substantial food taken before the journey, the glance of tenderness that gives courage and confidence. (p. 37)

I have walked through the world as if in a garden surrounded by walls. I have led a life of adventure on five continents, going from one edge to another... Yet the garden walls have only stepped back, and I am still imprisoned. But there will come a day when I will be able to sing my song of love and joy. All the barriers will come down. I will possess Infinity. (p. 38)

What was the prayer of faith of this contemporary saint like? He wrote:

> While attending the most distasteful play or watching the most inane movie, it is possible to pray a mechanical prayer to the rhythm of images or music, praying for the lead actors, for the director or the supporting cast. This prayer can be for the audience, which is amused or bored, or for the person sitting at your right or your left. Thus, the time which has passed will not be wasted. (p. 18)

In difficult times which required great faithfulness to the Lord, Guy de Larigaudie found strength in prayer:

> There are difficult times, when a temptation of sin takes hold of the flesh so strongly and irresistibly that one can only automatically repeat, while barely moving one's lips and almost not believing it, "My God, in spite of everything, I love You. Have pity on me."
>
> There are certain nights when seated in the back of a church...unable to pray, one can only repeat this simple phrase, which one holds on to like a lifesaver buoy that does not let one sink, "My God, in spite of everything, I love you." (pp. 13-14)
>
> While cutting down weeds with the aid of a riding crop, chewing a small blade of grass, shaving in the morning, one can simply tirelessly repeat to God that you love Him very much...Reminisce by singing to yourself about your past life and your dreams of the future and, in this way, speak to God through your singing. And speak to Him also

while dancing for joy in the sun, on the beach, or skiing in the snow. Have God always close to you, like a friend in whom you can trust. (p. 14)

I have become so accustomed to the presence of God in me that I always have a prayer deep in my heart, which rises to my lips like a blossom. This barely conscious prayer does not stop even when dozing to the gentle rocking of a train or the hum of a ship's turbine, even in the rapture of my body or soul, or in the bustle of the city or when my mind is occupied in an absorbing task. Somewhere, deep within me, is an infinitely calm and transparent water that cannot be affected either by shadows or whirlpools from the surface. (p. 36)

My whole life has been one long search for God. Everywhere, at any hour, in all places of the world, I have looked for His trace and presence. Death will be for me only a wonderful release from the leash. (p. 36)

CHAPTER FIFTEEN

LOVE AS
THE ACTUALIZATION
OF FAITH

At His Ascension, Christ assured us that He would remain with us for all time, until the end of the world (cf. Mt 28:20). He has remained not only in the Church, and not only in the Eucharist that is the making present of His redeeming works, but **He has also remained in our neighbors** with whom He identifies Himself, "Whatever you did for one of these least brothers of mine, you did for me" (Mt 25:40). Thanks to the presence of our neighbors, daily life becomes a challenge to our faith, since it is faith that allows us to look at the world as through the eyes of Christ and to perceive the presence of God hidden in another person.

Faith works "through love" (Gal 5:6), and in love it finds its fullness of life. Faith invites us to enter into "communion" with God and our brothers. God reveals His love (Greek: *agape*) to us, which we accept through faith, so that in turn we may pass it on to others. John Paul II has said it is in love that entrusting oneself through faith to God attains its true character and the dimension of a reciprocal gift.

AGAPE

Two basic kinds of bonds exist between people, and there are two concepts of love that correspond to them. The first ancient concept, given to us by Plato, defines love with the word *eros*; the second, which Christianity presents, is love as defined in the Greek language by the term *agape*. Eros and agape are two types of love that are the foundation of two different bonds between people. Plato's eros is love for that which one deems worthy of love. This is emotional love. If someone or something suits you because of an attractive, aesthetic appearance, or if you like being with someone or owning something, all of this arises solely from your purely natural feelings, and this is Plato's eros. You love something that gives you pleasure, that comforts you. This is an egocentric love because it always **concentrates on you**, on **your** pleasure.

This love, despite its inadequacies and limitations, and in spite of its self-interest and impermanence, should not be condemned or destroyed. It is connected with the natural order of things originating from God but it is blemished by Original Sin. It should be purified and transformed into a supernatural love that is essentially connected with a life of grace and is, according to the Gospel as well as to the thoughts of St. Paul, the reflection of God's own love. This love is described by the famous words of St. Paul in his Letter to the Corinthians, "Love is patient, love is kind…It does not seek its own interests, it is not quick-tempered, it does not brood over injury…It bears all things, believes all things, hopes all things" (1 Cor 13:4-7). This kind of love in the original Greek language is defined by the term agape. In the Christian concept, God is agape – a love that descends on a person and loves that which is unworthy of love. This is a spontaneous love that imparts itself only because it is love. Agape is a gratuitous love that encompasses a person. It sometimes seems to us that we should win God over, that we should merit His love. But He loves you because you are His child, not because you are worthy. **Agape is love that creates, that loves you not because you are worthy of being loved, but to make you worthy of it.** Agape desires to create an ever-increasing good in you. Someone who has received special graces from God is surprised that these graces have been bestowed on him. But agape love descends on the unworthy – descends on us all – because we are all unworthy and we all need this creative love that creates good. The anguish for God, who is love, is that He cannot pour out His love fully, that he cannot boundlessly flood the human soul with this love. God is continuously seeking open hearts on which He may pour out His infinite love without limits.

To every loving mother, her child will always be the most beautiful, even if the ugliest, because this is her own child. Is it important how many flaws you have? Maybe you have a multitude of them; maybe they depress you; maybe you cannot stand them any longer. **But God wants to embrace you with His love;** He wants to descend upon you, to create love in you in order to make you, who are sinful and unworthy, a masterpiece of His love.

Agape love, which descends upon you from God, and that you accept through faith, cannot be kept within you. Love, as a value, as a good, must be poured out and must be passed on. Agape is Christ who lives in you and wants to love others through you and in you. A person gifted with agape love, a selfless love, begins to give love. Strictly speaking, it is Christ within him who begins to love others. Agape is not so much an emotional love as a love from the will, which wants to bestow good on others. The bonds it creates between people can last even after death. It is not important who the other person is – ugly or pretty, pleasant or unpleasant, full of flaws and sin, or not. What is important is that the agape love wants to love him so that he may become a better person. That agape love, which grows within you because of Christ descending into your heart, is often expressed in trivial things, in gestures or looks. It is very important for you to express this love in the warmth of your look, in the acceptance, in the wonder, and in the continual, friendly welcome of another person.

THE ROLE OF FEELINGS

Agape is not only a love that creates, but it is also a love that forms a communion, a community of people. Contact between people is often a question of feelings. There are three basic kinds of emotional human relationships. The first kind could be an emotional relationship driven by **positive feelings**. If someone is dear to you and appeals to you, then you like them and want to be with them. We can experience such positive feelings in relation to God as well as to man. For example, you might feel content with God. Sometimes a person is "beside himself with joy" when he remains in emotional contact with God for hours, days, months. Positive feelings may flood the human soul. In the second kind of emotional relationship, positive feelings fade and a certain kind of **emotional emptiness** arises, nothing attracts you to a particular person. This may either happen suddenly or it may be a gradually increasing process. From a psychological point of view, it can then be said that there is a certain emotional disintegration. In the third kind of relationship, the most difficult one, **negative feelings** appear. Feelings of dislike may arise toward a person, as well as toward matters concerning God. The latter often occurs during periods of purification. Something may "push you away" from church, you may feel a reluctance toward going to Confession or Holy Communion, and you may have difficulties in your contact with God. Similarly, negative feelings may arise toward another person. Suddenly someone who was your close friend starts to irritate and repulse you.

Human bonds based on positive feelings are natural bonds. These kinds of feelings and bonds may arise within every group of people, even among criminals. There can be bonds among colleagues. We often meet people that are perfectly matched in the sense of natural bonds because of their common interests. However, natural positive feelings are by no means lasting. For example, these feelings may occur at the beginning of a marriage and then later fade. What happens when they fade? A crisis develops, caused by the growing emotional emptiness that is difficult to endure.

In relation to God, this will be a certain kind of dryness: *I do not feel anything in my contact with God; nothing draws me to prayer, to Confession, or to the Eucharist.* A similar crisis can appear because of a lack of feelings toward another person, when suddenly nothing draws you to someone who was previously close to you. Then there arises a specific emptiness in relation to friends and acquaintances.

Finally, the third very difficult situation occurs when there appears an emotional dislike toward matters relating to God or a dislike for another person. In this circumstance sometimes even heroism is needed to overcome oneself. However, it is then, **when a natural bond ceases, breaks down to some degree, or is at least reduced, that an opportunity arises for a supernatural bond to appear or to be deepened.**

It can occur in a marriage that a couple is well-matched, like two pieces of a split brick that fit together perfectly. In the light of faith, this is not an ideal situation because it is only a purely natural harmony of positive feelings. This is not yet Christian love, agape love, which has to be worked at. It may occur similarly with the children in a family. They do not have to be in full harmony, and it is not the point for there to be no problems with them. The point is that they try to love each other despite their faults and different individual characteristics, not that they be in total harmony with one another.

THE CRISIS OF NATURAL BONDS

Every community of people, whether in marriage, friendship, or in any group, if based solely on natural bonds, does not have much chance of survival. Someday, sooner or later, it has to either break down or attain a higher level of existence. Looking at this in the light of faith, it can be said that it is a good thing that these kinds of crises occur in our lives. It is good when suddenly someone becomes less pleasant, less liked by us, because by this we get an exceptional opportunity. Then the call of Christ to live by the Gospel becomes particularly significant. This also occurs in relation to God during purifications, which are sometimes intense and rapid. Then you may not feel any contact with God; you may find that you do not love Him at all; that something actually repels you from Him; and yet, in spite of this, you still try to be faithful to Him. How very precious Confession then is when you have no desire to go. And how very precious the Eucharist is when nothing draws you to it, and yet you go because you know that it is He, Christ who loves you, who is there waiting for you. How much more effort you must then make; **your gift of self increases to the extent of the lack of natural bonds**. How good it is that crises occur among us, that sometimes there are misunderstandings in marriage, that children sometimes fight among themselves because they do not get along with each other. These are the cracks, the fissures, that enable the birth or deepening of supernatural bonds and supernatural love. It is this very love that is the work of Christ, that is everlasting if allowed to develop. Only this kind of love is strong – strong by the power of Christ, by the power of God. A marriage that is strong in God is a marriage that has gone through this type of disintegration and was able to reintegrate on a higher level. Blessed is each person who has undergone a similar difficult experience with

God, who did not betray Him and remained faithful to Him, because it was then that His love really took root.

In all of this there is a kind of great hope, especially for those who worry that it is sometimes so hard for them. It is not always easy to get along with another person. Sometimes it seems that someone does everything to repulse us. But it is then that this person becomes a special grace for us, because he brings with him the call to transcend the natural bond and move toward a supernatural bond, toward agape. From the point of view of faith, people that we like the least are the most precious for us because they present the greatest chance for our attitudes to be polarized, for us to realize that to love is not the same as to like.

TO ALLOW CHRIST TO LOVE IN US

The distinctiveness of Christian love is Christocentrism in both meanings of this word. First of all, Christ is the most perfect and unique example of love. **You should love as He loves**, "I give you a new commandment: love one another. As I have loved you, so you also should love one another" (Jn 13:34). But for you to be able to love as Christ does, you have to discover, through faith, His true image as shown by the revealed Word. It is not sufficient to learn about Christ in theory. It is only with the growth of faith that love will grow in you, that there will be a growth of the existential bond with the ideal example of love, which is the person of Jesus Christ Himself. Through faith, which allows you to listen intently to the revealed Word and adhere to the person of Christ, you will come to know Him who is the example of love, and you will desire to love just as He loved, as He loved to the end. Through faith you will start to absorb His thoughts and desires; you will think as He does, desire as He does, and love as He does.

Secondly, **Christian love is the love of Christ in us**. He is our Way, our Truth and our Life. He is the One who thinks, prays, lives, and loves in us with His love. The magnitude of our love is determined by the greatness of our faith that allows us to share in the life of God. The imitation of Christ is not as much to literally follow the example of His deeds as it is an adherence to Christ through faith, so that His will becomes our will, so that His life could continuously be expressed in our lifestyle. To entrust ourselves to Christ through faith means to accept His descending love, so that we allow Him to love us, so that He Himself can love others in us and through us. Faith allows us to adhere to Christ, to entrust and devote ourselves to Him in such a way that faith becomes one with love and trust. Faith, which permeates the entire Christian existence, contains within itself hope and love as two forms of the actualization of faith.

It is not easy to love someone whom we dislike. That is why we must open ourselves to Christ and feel like helpless children in the face of the crushing waves of negative feelings. We must have the attitude of a child who is helpless when faced with matters that pertain to God, people, our surroundings and the environment. This is an attitude of trust-filled faith, believing that Jesus Himself will come and love in us even those whom we do not like. It is this kind of attitude that will enable us to come to agape love. Ultimately, when negative feelings increase in us, or at least when positive feelings fade, only Christ is able to love in us. Thanks to Him, our will should have freedom from emotions, or at least it should strive to have this kind of freedom. His presence in us brings us conversion; it liberates us and grants us grace, thus equally grants us freedom. However, this Presence is actualized to the extent of humility in us, to the extent that we are little and helpless before God. Only when we are like this are we able to accept the love of Jesus through faith. Hence, in this way of understanding, the appearance of a difficulty in our relationship with people is a chance to open ourselves to grace, to the love of Jesus. He descends upon us as divine agape when He sees how helpless we are with our feelings while, at the same time, we look for everything to come from Him.

Christ, who descends into your heart, wants to love; He wants to give Himself to others and desires their good. He wants to love more and more, and He desires the greatest good for others, which in the light of faith means desiring their sanctity. If you love someone, and worry only about their material, temporal matters, then you must realize that you actually lack authentic love. It is not sufficient to be concerned about the affairs of temporal life, about education, health, and material wealth. **You can love fully only when you yourself long for sanctity and when you desire to engraft this longing into others.**

YOU CANNOT LOVE PEOPLE IF YOU DO NOT LOVE GOD

The truth that Christ loves another person through you implies that you cannot love a person without loving God.

You alone are unable to love. It is Christ who loves in you. By loving Christ and becoming open to Him – becoming open to the divine agape that descends upon you – you allow Him to love you and to love others through you. Opening yourself to the descent of Christ, whether it is through the Holy Sacraments or in prayer, allows you to love others. **You can give Christ to others to the extent that you accept Him and to the extent that you allow Him to encompass you.** To love another person means to impart Christ to him. You cannot impart that which you do not have. The more you love God and accept Him in this love by allowing Him to live and act in you, the more capable you are of loving others.

To love means to give oneself, to impart good to others. However, it is not sufficient to give only material goods; in the light of faith, spiritual goods are more important. If you do not give them to those close to you, then a specific spiritual "theft," a specific spiritual "harm," takes place. Surely they have a right to these spiritual goods. Those around you have a right for you to become a pure channel of grace for them as you grow in sanctifying grace and in striving toward sanctity. Your growth in sanctity becomes, in the light of faith, the most precious gift for those close to you. You have to question your love, you have to stand in the truth and ask yourself whether you really love. You are most certainly convinced that you love your child because, not only are you concerned about temporal matters, but you also pray for him. Yet the value and efficacy of your prayer depends not on feelings, but on the greatness of sanctifying grace, on the greatness of your faith and love of God. If there is no spiritual life in you, if there is a lack of growth in faith and in

God's love, then, in the spiritual sense, you become a "thief" to those around you.

A mother who is a "lukewarm" Christian and has not adhered to Christ through faith should realize that, because she has not come to love Christ, she does not fully love her child. In not receiving Holy Communion, she also deprives her child, who is precious to her, of special graces. Not being aware of it, she is stealing the graces that he would receive thanks to her Holy Communions. This is because every participation in the Eucharist and in the sacrament of Penance, every time you receive one of the other sacraments, and every one of your prayers are always the giving of good to others due to the "system of connected vessels." These connected vessels are a system of our tight mutual bonds within the Mystical Body of Christ. You love your husband, son, daughter, parents, those close to you or those who are not, to the extent that you yourself are converted to God, to the extent that you strive for sanctity, and to the extent that you no longer live, but that Christ lives in you. He, who is the only love and only good, desires to love you boundlessly and is always seeking souls that He may flood with the boundless ocean of His love. One cannot love man without loving God. In fact, only saints truly love others; they are the ones who have fully opened themselves to Christ and in whom Christ can fully live and love.

SELF-ACTUALIZATION IN CHRIST

Psychology tells us of an *ideal I* and an *actual I*. All of us have some idea of who we would want to be, the image and likeness we would like to bring about in ourselves. These desires are a reflection of the ideal I. On the other hand, the real I can sometimes be so repulsive that some are irritated or even maddened by it. This is not the proper attitude. However, this proves that man does not want to be who he really is, that he has his idealized I, and that he desires to be different – to be more like the ideal image of himself.

If you open yourself to Christ through faith, He becomes your way, your truth, and your life (cf. Jn 14:6). He then starts to show you your ideal I and at the same time makes it a reality. Christ alone will bring about your self-actualization.

In a believer, the image of his ideal I will be perfected along with his growth in spiritual life and with the development of his identification with Christ. Coming to know Christ and adhering to Him gives rise to a desire within us to identify ourselves with Him. Christ then becomes our ideal example of a person, our ideal I. Growing in faith and grace causes a clarification of our ideal I, because then Christ grants us ever more supernatural light and reveals Himself to us all the more fully.

We are all destined "to be conformed to the image of his Son" (Rom 8:29); thus, only Christ can be our **true** example of an ideal person. As the image of our ideal I becomes more similar to the image of Christ, **we approach the truth**; for it is Christ Himself who becomes our way and truth. Moreover, He Himself imparts strength to our will so that we can form our real I following the example of our ideal I.

Each of us brings about our own self only when we love. I can actualize my self thanks to the ones whom I love. Such is God's economy, and such is my psychological structure. None of us can bring about our self without a relationship with another person. Without this relationship we will never fully be ourselves. Sometimes in our interaction with another person, everything seems almost perfect, and then we do not see the need for heroism. However, sometimes a person can put us into a situation such that, without heroism, there would only remain that which contradicts love. During World War II, people were often in situations that called for heroic love – strike, or you will be beaten; kill, or you will be killed. This was an exceptional circumstance, but God will also call us to love at great cost in less dramatic situations. We will then be convinced that we are unable to love, and it will be easier for us to understand the profound sense of Christ's words, "I am the vine, you are the branches. Whoever remains in me and I in him will bear much fruit, because without me you can do nothing" (Jn 15:5). Without Christ **we can do nothing**. It is Christ who is our life. Without Him, we become like the branch that withers when cut from the vine. A person cannot actualize himself without Christ.

Our self-actualization is brought about to the extent that we open ourselves to Christ, **to the extent that we allow Him to love from within us – that we allow God Himself to live in us.** If you would fully open yourself to Christ, then you could say, as St. Paul said, "Yet I live, no longer I, but Christ lives in me" (Gal 2:20). Christ really does have such an unusual desire: **He wants to love with a love proper to each of us**; He wants to have as many faces as there are people on earth.

The Church teaches that there is no love without a cross to bear. In order to be able to love another person, my self must be crucified. However, I am not able to accept this without grace. Only grace will make me capable of this. Grace acts in such a way within us that it is Christ Himself who partakes in our *I want*, in our human *I want to love; I want to choose good*. "For God is the one who, for his good purpose, works in you both to desire and to work" (Phil 2:13).

Our will, by which we can choose love and goodness, is weak. The human will is too weak to choose that which is difficult, that which requires the opposing of one's own egoism. If someone has not yet experienced this, then it is certain that someday he will be convinced that he really is unable to love, that his egoism is unable to die. It is only through love that each one of us fully becomes a human being.

Love is an act of will; it is our desire to bestow on others what is good. For example, we know that each of us may want good for others at five, seventy, or as much as one hundred per cent. But if we have only a ten percent desire for love to be brought about, this is not sufficient to form harmony among people, not sufficient for the process of the **integration of people** to begin, and not sufficient to love as Christ loved. However, my *I want* can be magnified by the grace of Christ so that I will start to want to fulfill Christ's commandment, "As I have loved you, so you also should love one another" (Jn 13:34), not at the ten percent level, but at seventy percent, or even higher. This reveals the life of Christ in us.

Perceiving Christ in another person in no way diminishes the value of that person. By loving Christ, I also love that person. It is because of Christ that another person begins to fascinate me and becomes increasingly interesting and more beautiful to me. Christ, when entering the realm of a person's will, makes the person desire good all the more. He makes more and more goodness present in that person. This is that person's good, because an accepted grace remains the good of a person, even though it is simultaneously the good of Christ. Christ enters one's life in such a perfect way that it is **He who loves another person with my love, and I who love with His love.** There is no separation or alienation here. On the contrary, thanks to Christ being in me, I become my true self – I love and I grow in love.

If Christ becomes my ideal I, then my self-actualization is brought about. On the other hand, when I sin, when I say *no* to Christ, I rob myself of my own I. Then I become even less myself. When I sin, I close myself off from Christ; I am isolated. If I close myself to Christ I become sad, depressed, and angry. However, I do not want to be like this; this is not my ideal I. It is Christ who is the ideal I – yours and mine – of each one of us. At the same time, it is He who actualizes the ideal I in each one of us. That is why He assumes so many faces. This wonderful reality confirms the words of Christ, "I am the way and the truth and the life" (Jn 14:6).

Our self-actualization is brought about through our living in the truth and through our responding to the divine call to love. Without living in the truth, one cannot talk about love in the supernatural sense. This love is the love of Christ Himself in us. And Christ lives within us to the extent that we beckon Him because we see ourselves in truth, that is, as we come to know our weakness. He lives within us to the extent that we want Him to be our life. A person is not capable of doing supernatural good by himself. The Church does not say that human nature is corrupt; nevertheless, we should be aware that we ourselves are not capable of doing supernatural good, that we are incapable of loving. We ourselves are not capable of undertaking this unusually difficult divine call, especially the call to love our neighbor, which sometimes actually requires heroism. Christ, in His conversation with the rich man, said, "Why do you call me good? No one is good but God alone" (Mk 10:18). Everything that is good in us originates in God: "What do you possess that you have not received?" (1 Cor 4:7).

We have to continually return to these words because self-actualization in Christ is impossible without living in the truth. Christ said about Himself, "For this I was born and for this I came into the world, to testify to the truth" (Jn 18:37). **God is particularly sensitive to the truth.** Ascribing human characteristics to God, it could be said that truth is God's "weak point." If you are to be conformed to the image of Christ, then there can be no falsehood in you. Christ, who identifies with truth, is uncompromising toward falsehood and pride, toward our claiming His work in us as our own. The more divine graces that we credit to ourselves, the greater is our foolishness. God, in order to save us from this, will have to limit His graces.

Humility is fundamental to our self-actualization. Humility is so important because **God is ready to give everything to a person who credits nothing to himself.** If you live in the truth and acknowledge that you can do nothing without Christ, it is as if you are beckoning to Him: *Come and live in me.* It is only then that Christ comes.

In order not to credit the works of Christ to yourself, try to repeat as often as you can: *It is thanks to You, Christ, that I am myself; it is thanks to You that my spouse is so appealing; thanks to You that the people I meet are so good.* This will be a sign of your humility. Everything that appeals to me in another person belongs to Christ and, at the same time, belongs to that person. If we were to suppose that someone who fascinates us with his supernatural good is himself worthy of admiration, then this would be submitting to an illusion. Every one of us will be convinced, someday, of how weak and sinful we are. Meanwhile, Christ wants to create a masterpiece out of us – out of you – that will amaze others. Then you will become more and more yourself and, simultaneously, Christ will grow in you.

Every one of the saints brought about the image of Christ in themselves in a different way. It is quite extraordinary that we have so many different kinds of saints. In the history of the Church in Poland, St. Queen Jadwiga (Hedwig) was almost like an *arbiter elegantiarum* – she had unique taste not just in terms of aesthetics; she fascinated others with her intelligence and the level of her spiritual and intellectual attributes.[66] On the other hand, we can learn from St. Benedict Labres who died as a pauper and beggar. We can also learn from St. Camille de Lellis who, as a young man, gambled with cards, was a rogue, and led a life that was probably worse than the life of soldiers thrown out of the

---

[66] *Arbiter elegantiarumn:* an authority in matters of taste.—Ed.

French Foreign Legion. Once, when he was already an alcoholic, he saw a monk and suddenly a ray of hope appeared in him, *Surely even I can be a different person.* Later, when he lost at cards and was forced to beg, covering his face with a scarf, the desire to stop all this was once again renewed. He then understood that what he was doing was degrading, that he was not himself, that he was a caricature of a man. He started to dream that he could be a normal man. He decided to be converted. It was then that Christ brought about St. Camille's self-actualization. Christ made not only a normal person out of him, but He made a masterpiece and led him to sanctity.

This is how Christ treats us. He does this because He wants to become **everything** for us – our love, our way, our truth, and our life.

FAITH SHARING GUIDELINES

RECOMMENDED GUIDELINES NEXT PAGE

The "Decalogue for Faith Sharing" is recommended by the Families of Nazareth Movement USA for use with this book at small group meetings. *The Gift of Faith* is known to help the reader recognize God's loving Presence in their everyday life.

RECOMMENDED PRAYER AFTER SHARING

The prayer below is recited by an individual at the conclusion of their personal sharing. This becomes a signal to others that they may now share. It allows a person to express their thoughts completely without interruption.

PRAYER AFTER SHARING

Thank you, God, for allowing me to see the truth about my weaknesses and how it calls upon the abyss of your merciful love.

Decalogue for Faith Sharing

1. **Meetings are led by the Holy Spirit.**

2. **The purpose of the meeting is:**
   - to become aware of my weaknesses and the truth of being loved by God.
   - to respond to the desire to deepen my faith.
   - to be open to others, my brothers and sisters in the group.
   - to share different experiences of my faith and how God is present in my life.

3. **When I go to the meeting, I will pray to God for others and myself.**
   - The prayer of empty hands or that of the tax collector is recommended.

4. **I will remember that I am God's child** who has the right to trust and await miracles.

5. **As a participant in our meeting I will:**
   - serve others and not count my own merits.
   - create the atmosphere of calm, focus/concentration and openness.
   - not impose on others my ways of thinking, reacting and perceiving.
   - avoid giving advice or solving others' problems.
   - speak from my personal "I" rather than use terms such as "you, we, us, people, we should, others do this."
   - avoid discussion and criticism.

6. **By keeping what is shared in the meeting confidential,** I will preserve each participant's freedom to share openly and protect their dignity as a child of God.

7. **I will not be afraid of moments of silence,** since I or somebody else may need time to reflect. Moments of silence provide us with unique opportunities for prayer and entrustment to God.

8. **I will remember to attentively listen** to what my brother or sister is saying in order to help them in the process of sharing.

9. **When I give a witness talk or share my faith, God's grace** is not only given to me but it is being multiplied and given to others.

10. **Above all, God expects from me humility and openness.** Even one person who is humble and open to God can create an appropriate climate during a given meeting that will spread to all participants. The most important and desirable goal is not the format of the meeting, but it is to be open to God's grace and presence.

Prayer After Sharing: ***Thank you, God, for allowing me to see the truth about my weaknesses and how it calls upon the abyss of your merciful love.***

COMMUNION OF LIFE WITH CHRIST THROUGH MARY

IN THE ARMS OF MARY FOUNDATION
P. O. Box 271987
Fort Collins, CO 80527-1987

If **The Gift of Faith** has helped you to appreciate God's immense love and mercy, please consider donating to **In the Arms of Mary Foundation**, a 501(c)(3) organization, to help spread this spirituality (Communion of Life with Christ through Mary) throughout the USA and the world. Send donation checks or money orders payable to **In the Arms of Mary Foundation** to the address above.

For more information about the **In the Arms of Mary Foundation** or to obtain additional books, holy cards, free downloads of *Reflections on Faith* topics, or to sign up for the Quote of the Day, please visit the website at **www.IntheArmsofMary.org**.